# Undoing the Grade

# Undoing the Grade

Why We Grade, and How to Stop

Jesse Stommel

Undoing the Grade Copyright © 2023 by Jesse Stommel is licensed under a Creative Commons Attribution-NonCommercial 4.0 International License, except where otherwise noted.

Published by Hybrid Pedagogy, Inc. in Denver, CO.

# Contents

| | | |
|---|---|---|
| | Foreword<br>Martha Burtis | vii |
| | Author's Note | xiii |
| 1. | I Would Prefer Not To | 1 |
| 2. | An Introduction to Ungrading | 6 |
| 3. | Why I Don't Grade | 23 |
| 4. | Learning is Not a Mechanism | 33 |
| 5. | Love and Other Data Assets | 39 |
| 6. | If bell hooks Made a Learning Management System | 50 |
| 7. | Grades are Dehumanizing: Ungrading is No Simple Solution | 62 |
| 8. | How to Ungrade | 68 |
| 9. | Compassionate Grading Policies | 82 |
| 10. | Toward a Co-intentional Approach to Assessment | 91 |
| 11. | Ungrading for Equity | 100 |

| | | |
|---|---|---:|
| 12. | Frequently Asked Questions | *110* |
| 13. | What if We Didn't Grade?: A Bibliography | *122* |
| 14. | Do We Need the Word "Ungrading"? | *130* |
| | Afterword: The End of Grades<br>Sean Michael Morris | *141* |
| | Works Cited | *148* |

# Foreword

MARTHA BURTIS

While I have worked in and around higher education for all of my professional career, if I'm being honest, for the first ten years of that journey I didn't really think much about grades or assessment or the intersection of those issues with care, power, and, frankly, learning. Grades seemed to me like a necessary part of education, and grading seemed like the penance teachers must pay in order to participate in the community of education. My own relationship with grades as a learner had been fraught, but no more or less so than I suspect most people's, especially those people who tend to be drawn to a career in education: I sought good grades as a child because it was expected and they seemed like a mark of achievement. I experienced feelings of doubt and low self-worth when I struggled in classes and ended up with lower grades than I wanted. My parents at times encouraged me to get good grades; at other times, cajoled; a few times, punished. In retrospect, I could say that grades and my anxiety around them took a toll on my mental health in my adolescence and as I entered young adulthood. But, if I examine the situation more closely, it's pretty clear that the mechanism of that toll wasn't the grades; the grades were a symbol of something much more deeply insidious and complicated.

Two events converged in my life around the same time that made me begin to think about grading and assessment differently: first, after many years of working in the area of faculty and curricular support, I was asked to teach for the first time. I was no longer someone who dropped into the classroom to assist with an assignment or the person consulted about the design of a unit. In those roles, the question of grades never really entered the conversation. Occasionally, faculty would ask me the best way to assess a digital activity or for advice about using online assessment tools. I answered those as someone who had done research in these areas but had never had to make those critical decisions for my own teaching.

As a new teacher, almost every aspect was exciting and terrifying. But the prospect of figuring out the best way to grade my students was paralyzing. The class I was teaching, digital storytelling, fulfilled a *creative thought* general education requirement for my university. I knew that I wanted students to develop a better relationship with their own creativity. I wanted them to develop a creative habit. I wanted them to experiment, explore, share, make mistakes, and learn from those mistakes. I wanted them to choose work that was personally meaningful so that they would be inspired to take risks. But, I had no idea how to grade creativity, experimentation, exploration, sharing, mistake-making, or risk-taking. Grading those things felt like grading the abstract, like grading love or personhood. I did the best I could, and I muddled through, but even as the other aspects of teaching the course got easier each time, the question of assessing my students loomed over me, worried me, and, sometimes, sucked the joy out of teaching.

The second thing that happened around this time is that I became the parent of a school-aged child. My oldest entered kindergarten the same year that I started teaching. The one thing I wanted for them at that age was to love school. I wanted school and learning to be something they looked forward to. I wanted their teachers to be adults they trusted with their fragile, newly-developed sense of themselves as learners.

My child had entered kindergarten already an excellent reader and was immediately put into a "gifted" program called Junior Great Books. In theory, I liked the idea of the program. Kids were given stories and poems that were considered "literature" instead of reading stories developed for textbooks. They met once a week to read together and discuss the stories. I thought it would be like kindergarten book club. Then they started bringing packets home. It turned out every reading was accompanied with worksheets. I think the point of the worksheets was to give students a chance to respond creatively to the readings and gauge how well they were understanding what they read. I was less thrilled with this, but we plowed ahead. I encouraged my child to get them done, but I didn't look them over, review them, or concern myself too much with the "quality" of their worksheets. To be frank, they hated the worksheets. They barely spent any time on them. If they were asked to draw something, they didn't break out the 64 color box of crayons and create a masterpiece; they scribbled something with a pencil and got it done as quickly as possible. I didn't blame them.

I thought things were going fine with all of this. My child seemed to be thriving in kindergarten, making friends, learning new things, and, most importantly, looking forward to school each day. Then, one morning, as we waited for the school bus, out of nowhere they started to have a panic attack. There were tears, and when I dug further I discovered they had been told to redo a reading packet because their original work wasn't adequate. If they didn't redo it and turn it in today, the gifted teacher told them they were going to fail Junior Great Books. Let me repeat that: The gifted teacher told my kindergartener they would get an F in reading if they didn't redo a worksheet. Up until that moment, I didn't even think my child knew what an "F" was.

The confluence of these two events, my teaching and my child entering kindergarten, brought into stark focus that there was something wrong with what we were doing in our schools. It all seemed to keep coming back to grades. A few years later, when I was introduced to the concept of ungrading by Jesse Stommel, I embraced the idea. I rejiggered my classes around the practice of regular self-evaluation and open conversation about the purpose and meaning of our work. Since then, I've never taught a traditionally graded class again, and I never will.

This is the point when I should tell you that in this book you should be prepared to encounter pages of wisdom about how to ungrade: the practices, tools, techniques and approaches you will need. That you will come away feeling more confident about your ability to do this. That if anyone can teach you how to ungrade, it is Jesse Stommel. But I'm not going to tell you that, because after years of grappling with these issues and figuring out how to make ungrading work for me and my classes, I've learned one thing: it isn't actually about grades. It is about the things that grades stand in for. It is about the class you teach that sits beneath the grades.

Ten years ago when my child cried on the driveway waiting for the bus, the tears weren't about getting an F. The tears were about the frustration of being asked to do mindless busy work that interrupted her relationship with the stories she was trying to understand and enjoy. And six years ago, when I discovered ungrading and changed assessment in my classes, it worked because I was already teaching in ways that adapted to these practices. You can't ungrade away a broken assignment. You can't ungrade away a lack of care for your students. You can't ungrade away pedagogy that is rooted in wielding power over students. More than anyone else, Jesse Stommel's words have taught me this: "We can't simply take away grades without re-examining all of our pedagogical approaches, and this work looks different for each teacher, in each context, and with each group of students."

## Author's Note

"It is true, we shall be monsters, cut off from all the world; but on that account we shall be more attached to one another." ~ Mary Shelley, *Frankenstein*

This book represents over 20 years of my thinking and writing about grades. Most of the text was written between 2017 and 2023, even as the ideas have germinated since 2001. Several of the pieces are brand new, published here for the first time, and others have been previously published in various book collections, academic journals, and on my personal blog. My own context is mostly higher education, but my hope is that this book is useful to teachers, librarians, staff, administrators, and students at all levels of education.

While I've edited the chapters to form a cohesive narrative and to reduce repetition, I've tried to take a light hand so that contradictions, evolutions, and seeming tangents in my thinking stay intact. A clear strand throughout the book is that teaching is idiosyncratic and happens differently for different teachers with different students at different institutions. Teaching also works differently *for me* on different days with different people, across years. Pedagogical thinking is necessarily messy, and so I wanted this book to embody that.

The works cited at the end of this book is a celebration of many of the folks who've influenced my thinking about grades and assessment. But there are a few people I want to especially acknowledge here.

My dad, my mom, and my brother have encouraged and challenged me from the start, each in their own ways.

Marty Bickman is the first teacher who challenged me to rethink what it meant to be a student, what it meant to be graded, what it meant to take ownership of my own learning.

R L Widmann is my teacher, my friend, and will be forever a part of my family. She taught me how to trust deeply, to front generosity, and to always ask hard questions with playfulness and curiosity.

Martha Burtis has changed my professional life in ways I barely have words for. She has helped me see the why of this work more than anyone else.

Sean Michael Morris has been my collaborator, my colleague, and my friend from the first day I started teaching. His sentences continue to inhabit my own.

I also want to thank my husband, Joshua Lee, and my daughter, Hazel Stommel-Lee for being marvelous. She still kicks my ass daily, and he gives me "I love you" eyes exactly when I need them.

Finally, all of the ideas here have come to life in conversation with the students I've worked with over the years. Their voices are the reason, the impetus, for my work.

# 1

# I Would Prefer Not To

Grades and assessment are elephants in almost every room where discussions of education are underway. While I'd prefer that grades would crawl back into the hole from which they came, my goal here is not to demonize assessment altogether but to dissect it — to cut right to its jugular: Where does assessment fail? What damage can it do and how can we mitigate that damage? What can't be assessed? Can we construct more poetic, less objective, models for assessment? In a system structured around standards and gatekeeping, when and how do we stop assessing?

Education needs more conscientious objectors. Taking a cue from one of my mentors, Martin Bickman, I've chosen never to grade, or at least almost never. While

I still submit grades at the end of a term, I've forgone grades on individual assignments for over 20 years, relying on qualitative feedback, peer review, and self-assessment. In "Ranking, Evaluating, and Liking: Sorting Out Three Forms of Judgment," Peter Elbow writes, "assessment tends so much to drive and control teaching. Much of what we do in the classroom is determined by the assessment structures we work under." My goal in eschewing grades has been to more honestly engage student work rather than simply evaluate it. Over many years, this has meant carefully navigating, and occasionally breaking, the sometimes draconian rules of more than a half-dozen institutions. And I've brought students into meta-level discussions about these choices and have encouraged the same sort of agency among them. I tell students they should consider our course a "busy-work-free zone." So, if an assignment doesn't feel productive, we find ways to modify, remix, or repurpose its instructions. And when our assessments fail us (as they often do), we don't change our learning, we find new tools for assessment.

Prior to the late 1700s, performance and feedback systems in U.S. education were idiosyncratic. The one-room schoolhouse called for an incredibly subjective, peer-driven, nontransactional approach to assessment. Throughout the nineteenth century, feedback systems became increasingly comparative, numerical, and standardized. Letter grades are a relatively recent phenomenon. They weren't widely used until the 1940s. In "Teaching More by Grading Less," Jeffrey Schinske and Kimberly Tanner cite the first "official record" of a grading system from Yale in 1785. The A–F system appears to have emerged in 1898 (with the E not disappearing until the 1930s), and the 100-point or percentage scale became common in the early 1900s. Even by 1971 only 67 percent of primary and secondary schools in the United States were using letter grades. The desire for uniformity across institutions was the primary motivator for the spread of these systems. (Schinske and Tanner)

A supposedly objective approach to grading was created so systematized schooling could scale — so students could be neatly ranked and sorted into classrooms with desks in rows in increasingly large warehouse-like buildings. And we've designed technological tools in the twentieth and twenty-first centuries, like MOOCs and machine grading, that have allowed us to scale even further, away from human relationships and care. In fact, the grade has been hard-coded into all our institutional and technological systems, an impenetrable phalanx of clarity, certainty, and defensibility.

In "Bartleby, the Scrivener," Herman Melville writes, "Nothing so aggravates an earnest person as a passive resistance." This is where our discussions must increasingly point, and not just with regard to assessment: how do we respond (both actively and passively) in the face of institutional demands we find unethical or pedagogically harmful? My reference to Bartleby here is more than a coy nod. With its incessant refrain, "I would prefer not to," the story critiques the changes in labor at the turn of the industrial age, the same changes still attempting to drive a very different educational landscape.

The answer to Bartleby today is not to throw up our hands, but rather to ask: "Okay, what would you prefer to do?" How can we work together to make a guide — a how-to manual for saying "I would prefer not to…" in a grander and more collective way? How can we turn a simple act of civil disobedience into a rallying cry? And when we put our tools down and stand back from the furnace, the letter press, or the paper mill, what will we turn to build instead?

If we object to the increasing standardization of education, how and where do we build sites of resistance? What strategies can we employ to protect ourselves and our students? What work-arounds can we employ as we build courage and community for structural change? What systems of privilege must we first dismantle? Finally, what kinds of assessment can or should we bring to our own strategies? If we write manifestos as a form of active resistance, how do we determine if they're working? As we organize, how do we measure the impact of our assembly? When we muster our pedagogy as a form of activism, how do we decide what counts as talk and what counts as action?

## 2

# An Introduction to Ungrading

The word "ungrading" means raising an eyebrow at grades as a systemic practice, distinct from simply "not grading." The word is a present participle, an ongoing process, not a static set of practices. Ungrading is a systemic critique, a series of conversations we have about grades, ideally drawing students into those conversations with the goal of engaging them as full agents in their own education. For me, there aren't a discrete set of best practices for ungrading, because different students learn in different ways at different times with different teachers in different disciplines at different institutions. So, the work of teaching, the work of reimagining assessment, is necessarily idiosyncratic.

Most important to the work of ungrading is that we start

by asking hard questions of our traditional approaches to assessment. There is a meaningful distinction to be made between grades and assessment. But at this moment, I'd say our approaches to assessment, our syllabi, the work we ask students to do, the shape of academic labour, is increasingly structured by grades. Rather than wondering at how we fit our pedagogies into systems that have become increasingly standardized and quantitative, we need to look askance at those systems, and find ways to dismantle barriers to teaching and learning.

Grades are inequitable. As they are increasingly centered at our institutions and within our educational technologies (like the learning management system), the inequities of grades are exacerbated, and our most marginalized students are further marginalized. This is one reason it's imperative that we rethink our approaches to assessment. The work of teaching is also precarious. The majority of teachers in higher education work in contingent, adjunct, or sessional positions, but increasingly the work of all teachers at all levels of education is not adequately supported and is structurally devalued. And so, teachers are rightfully skeptical of approaches to assessment that increase our labor with little benefit to us or students. Teachers are rightfully skeptical of approaches to assessment that create a culture of suspicion and competition, while further fracturing the already strained relationships between students, between teachers, and between students and teachers.

**Pivot /ˈpivət/**
: to turn on or as if on a pivot

In March of 2020, during the COVID-19 pandemic lockdown, there was what many people called a "pivot" to online learning. At the time, I immediately bristled at the choice of the word "pivot" to describe what was underway. It implied an easy turn, a shift supported by an already in place mechanism to facilitate it. And the implication was that we could and would just as easily "pivot" back after the pandemic lockdown was over. Many millions of teachers around the world were asked to suddenly reimagine the shape of their teaching, the location of their classrooms, and their approach to assessment. In higher education, especially in the U.S., most teachers have little to no formal preparation for the work of teaching, so the expectation that they would suddenly and implicitly understand how to teach in an online environment was unreasonable, if not absurd.

In April of 2020, I launched (with Sean Michael Morris) a series of open discussions about pedagogy, online learning, open education, and assessment, what we called "Open Online Office Hours." We invited anyone, working at all levels of education, teaching in any discipline, from anywhere in the world, to join us. Until the end of 2020, we held sessions every week, then every other week, with anywhere between 20 and 150 attendees. These were generative conversations, shaped by participants, without predetermined topics or outcomes. Assessment was often a central focus. There was considerable friction between what institutions were asking of teachers and the support institutions were offering those teachers. When it came to grades and assessment, there was a call for "compassion," but a simultaneous unwillingness to let go of the bureaucracies that shape what grading looks like at most educational institutions. Certainly, there was flexibility, to differing degrees at different schools, but rarely the necessary deep questioning of our assumptions about what education is for, how we can adequately prepare teachers for the work of teaching, and how we can meaningfully measure learning.

**Why Do We grade? Why Should We Stop?**

In *Pedagogy of the Oppressed*, Paulo Freire argues against the banking model of education, "an act of depositing, in which the students are the depositories and the teacher is the depositor." In place of the banking model, Freire's critical pedagogy advocates for "problem-posing education," in which a classroom or learning environment becomes a space for asking questions — a space of cognition not information. The fundamental inconsistency between critical pedagogy and standardized, quantitative assessment is the germ for much of my own interrogation of grades as a system. Ungrading is not ideologically neutral work; rather, it asks us to examine the structural inequities of education and to revise all our pedagogical approaches.

I start most conversations I have about grades and assessment with a series of big questions, deliberately delaying focus on specific practices:

- Who is assessment for?
- What's the difference between grading and feedback?
- Why do we grade?
- What would happen if we didn't grade?

There are no simple answers to these questions. Take the first question, "who is assessment for?" The answer is "for a lot of different people": accreditors, future employers, parents, graduate school admissions, other teachers, administrators, the teacher doing the grading, and the student. The needs of each of these audiences, and why they might be considering grades to begin with, is varied. (Whatever the needs of the other audiences, I'd say the needs of the student should be the primary focus of assessment.) Similarly, a question like, "what would happen if we didn't grade?," means something very different to a white male tenured full professor at an elite university than it does to a black transgender assistant professor at a small state school or to someone teaching in adjunct roles at several community colleges. Examining the structural inequities of grades requires that we also look at how compulsory grading intersects with the deeply problematic labor conditions of teachers. Too often, our educational systems reduce the work of teaching to the act of grading students, which instrumentalizes the work and leads to increased labor precarity.

Grades are the bureaucratic ouroboros of education. They are baked into our practices and reinforced by all our technological and administrative systems. Teachers continue to grade because so much of education is built around grades. But, if we can't "imagine the world as though it might be otherwise," as Maxine Greene would say, we are stuck with the bizarre customs and habits our institutions have adopted.

Historically, grades are more of an anomaly than anything else. They are a very recent technology. In North America, letter grades have an approximately 240-year history and weren't used with any regularity until the last 75 years (Schinske and Tanner). There is nothing normal, and certainly nothing inevitable, about grades. Standardized grades are a crude system invented for ranking students against one another with only a veneer of objectivity. Other technologies have been invented to "manage" the complexity (the fallibility) of grades (and assessment).

I would argue grading, by any of our conventional academic metrics, undermines the work. Research shows grades don't help learning and actually distract from other feedback/assessment. In "The Case Against Grades," Alfie Kohn writes, "when students from elementary school to college who are led to focus on grades are compared with those who aren't, the results support three robust conclusions: Grades tend to diminish students' interest in whatever they're learning ...; Grades create a preference for the easiest possible task ...; Grades tend to reduce the quality of students' thinking." In an educational system that increasingly centers grades and quantifiable outcomes, students work for the grade rather than for learning. Students ask questions like, "what are you looking for," "how many points is this worth," not "what will I do," but "what should I do, and how will it be graded?" The grade takes the complexity of human interaction within a learning environment and makes it machine-readable: A/

A-, A-/B+, D+, 97%, 59%, 18/20, 10/20, high first, low 2:1.

Learning, though, is not linear, and meaningful learning resists being quantified. Our assessment approaches should create space for learning, not arbitrarily delimit it. How, for example, can we "test" whether a student has had an epiphany? What standardized mechanism can account for a student learning experience we (and they) couldn't have anticipated? How can we evaluate (with a percentile) the significance of a student changing their mind about something? How can a letter grade account for the complexities of failure, struggle, or even success? These kinds of questions call for a pedagogy that is less algorithmic and more human, more subjective, more compassionate.

Ultimately, traditional grades are better at measuring and reinforcing compliance than they are at measuring or adequately communicating learning, engagement, or content knowledge.

**Start by Trusting Students**

An internet search for, "is cheating on the rise?," finds a half-dozen articles like one from *The Washington Post*, "Another Problem with Shifting Education Online: Cheating," which cites data about the rise of online cheating reported by ProctorU, whose revenue model hinges upon creating a culture of suspicion in education. As reported by *Vox*, the remote proctoring industry "is expected to grow from being a $4 billion market in 2019 to a nearly $21 billion market in 2023." This multi-billion dollar industry has a vested interest in maintaining a culture of suspicion and advancing a very narrow definition of academic integrity, for which the grade (or supposed "objectivity in grading") becomes a proxy.

Cheating is not, in fact, on the rise. In 1963, Bowers surveyed roughly 100 institutions and found that "75 percent of the surveyed students admitted to cheating at least once in their college careers." Rates of cheating have not changed all that much since then. McCabe, et. al.'s 2012 *Cheating in College* includes findings from 150,000 students recently surveyed, showing that "between 60 to 70 percent of respondents admitted cheating." (Lang, *Cheating Lessons*)

And so, cheating rates are flat, or on a slight decline, over the last 50-60 years. Meanwhile, Wiley surveyed 789 instructors for their 2020 report on "Academic Integrity in the Age of Online Learning": 93% of teachers felt students are more likely to cheat online than in-person. What follows in the report is a guide to discouraging academic misconduct without any sources for an actual rise in cheating beyond the imagination of those surveyed.

I certainly don't blame individual teachers for their perceptions about cheating. The work of teaching is hard, and educators put so much of ourselves into our work. Of course, we would be susceptible to the efforts of a multi-billion-dollar industry spending huge amounts on marketing to sell us a false narrative about students. As with so much of what we currently face in education, the problem is structural.

Over the last several years, I've been disturbed to watch institutions actually cut faculty development budgets while massively increasing spending on LMS contracts, proctoring solutions, plagiarism detection software, cameras in classrooms, and videoconferencing tools. There is no neat and tidy technological solution to the challenges we presently face in education.

Cheating is a pedagogical issue, not a technological one. We can design proactively and together with students, rather than relying on cruel, racist, ableist, surveillance tech that creates a culture of suspicion which interferes with good pedagogies.

## Designing for Care

I haven't put a grade on a single piece of student work in over 20 years. This practice continues to feel like an act of personal, professional, and political resistance.

When I first started pushing back against grades over 20 years ago, I was inspired by one of my teaching mentors, Martin Bickman, who taught a graduate course called "Theory and the Teaching of Literature." As he writes,

> The course was built around a beginning undergraduate course that we all taught together. We met for the hour immediately after each undergraduate class to share our perceptions and analyses of it, to relate it to theories we had read or formulated ourselves, and to plan the upcoming class in the light of all this.

We gave no grades to the undergraduates in our co-taught course, aside from final grades based on their own self-evaluations. During that same semester, I was also teaching freshman composition, the first course I'd taught as instructor of record. I didn't put grades on student work in that course either. As I wrote in a piece for *The Chronicle of Higher Education*, I learned, from my first semester of teaching, "to constantly inspect and wonder at even the smallest of choices we make as teachers."

My assessment approach focuses on self-evaluation and metacognition. I ask students to write process letters about their work, and I ask them to reflect frequently on their own progress and learning. The most authentic assessment approaches, in my view, are ones that engage students directly as experts in their own learning.

I offer feedback with words and sentences and

paragraphs, or by just talking to students, rather than using a crude system for quantitative evaluation. I also encourage students to see their peers as a primary audience for their work, rather than just me. Students in my classes give themselves a grade at the end of the term. In an introductory course, like Digital Studies 101 or freshman composition, I begin with more frequent self-reflections and more directive prompts. In advanced courses, I might have students do a midterm self-reflection with directive prompts and an open-ended final self-reflection. I sometimes ask students to blog their way through a course, reflecting constantly (but less formally) on their process.

A midterm self-reflection might begin with questions like,

> What aspects of the course have been most successful for you so far? What thing that you've learned are you most excited about? What challenges have you encountered?

I usually ask students to quote from or link to examples of their work right within the self-reflection. I don't necessarily respond to every self-reflection (especially in a large class), so one of the last questions invites students to ask for particular kinds of feedback. A final self-reflection will either include a shorter series of questions that build upon the midterm self-reflection, or it might have a single open-ended prompt, such as:

> Write me a short letter that reflects on your work in this class. Consider the work you did on the final project, your work earlier in the term, the feedback you offered your peers on their work, and how you met your own goals. Include links to examples of your work. Did you miss any significant work? Is there anything you are particularly proud of? What letter grade would you give yourself?

Taking grades at least partly off the table means I have a whole different set of conversations with students than I otherwise would. We all (students and teachers) bring anxiety about grades into the classroom with us. Ungrading doesn't mean we can blink our eyes and those anxieties go away. Instead, we have to do the hard work of reflecting on our own learning, on our own teaching, talking about processes, not just products.

In *Education for Critical Consciousness*, Paulo Freire describes "an education of 'I wonder,' instead of merely 'I do.'" I'd argue that the kinds of relationships necessary for the work of education are not possible unless we work actively to decenter grades and draw students in as co-authors of our assessment practices.

## Small Things We Can Do Tomorrow to Start Ungrading

The notion of best practices does harm. In *Teaching to*

*Transgress*, bell hooks writes about bringing our full selves to the classroom, and creating space for students to bring their full selves. But each teacher, each student, encounters the classroom differently. hooks writes, "any radical pedagogy must insist that everyone's presence is acknowledged" (8). The work of learning is idiosyncratic, embodied. The work of teaching is idiosyncratic, embodied. Power flows in specific and complicated ways in education. Pedagogical practices that work for a disabled, queer white teacher may not work in the same way for an able-bodied, indigenous, woman of color. And "what works" will shift from one year to the next, one institution to the next, one geography to the next, one group of students to the next.

Grading is so ingrained in our educational systems that small acts of pedagogical disobedience can't do enough to change the larger (and hostile) culture of grading and assessment. The work has to be less about shifting policies and more about building community. We can't instantly manifest a learning environment entirely free of grades and quantitative assessment, but we can create safe spaces for students to ask critical questions about grades and about how school works. We can create safe spaces for teachers to experiment boldly with their pedagogical approaches in collaboration with students.

How do we begin this work?

**Talk with students about grades.** Demystifying grades (and the culture around them) helps students develop a sense of ownership over their own education. I spend an entire week of a 15-week course on metacognition, talking with students about how we learn and what shapes that learning takes. We foreground thinking and active discussion of bias and privilege. We connect this to the rest of the course by also discussing ways of knowing in the specific discipline we're working within.

Ungrading shifts the focus away from purely extrinsic motivation and insidious hierarchical relationships between teachers and students by dismantling structures that pit us against each other and structures that encourage competition over collaboration.

**Investigate other approaches to alternative assessment.** I don't use the word "ungrading" as an umbrella term for all alternative approaches to assessment, rather it acts as one possible entry point into a long history of push back on traditional grades. Entire institutions (like Evergreen State College and University of California Santa Cruz) have foregone traditional grades in favor of narrative evaluation. Some of the other alternative approaches I discuss later in this book include:

<u>Minimal Grading</u>: Moving away from 1000- or 100-point scales and toward 3- (done, excellent, needs

revision), 2- (done, needs revision), and 1-point scales (done, not done), using fewer demarcations to make grading "simpler, fairer, clearer." (Elbow)

Contract Grading: Offering clear expectations about what is required for each grade with goalposts that don't unexpectedly shift. Labor-based contract grading specifically emphasizes process over product, labor over subjective "judgments of quality" (Inoue).

Authentic Assessment: Having students do work for real-world audiences, while focusing more intently on intrinsic motivation, and drawing students into the design of assignments / assessments.

Process Letters and Self-evaluation: Asking students to reflect on their work and offering feedback on those reflections. Students help guide the grading of their own work.

**Start with "hello, how are you."** So much of our teaching gets reduced to a stack of bureaucratic documents: lesson plans, syllabi, assignment sheets, course descriptions. Students often encounter those documents before they encounter us or each other. In response, we can literally put the words "hello, how are you" at the top of our syllabi or on the front page of our course site, or we can find other ways to explicitly front our own humanity and the humanity of our students. For example, move statements about basic needs, accessibility, disability accommodation, and mental health from the end of our syllabi to the beginning, and write those statements in the first person. (If our institution requires its own boiler-plate language, we can include that, but not at the expense of our own care and clear expression of how students can ask for help.)

And, finally, **don't replace visible goalposts with invisible ones.** To the extent that we can remove (or decenter) grades, we have to be sure we aren't just shifting the goalposts for students, replacing clear policies with "hidden curriculum." The problem of removing grades without changing any of our other pedagogies is not that we end up removing the ground underneath students' feet. Grades are not and have never been a stable or supportive ground beneath students' feet. But we can't simply remove grades without actively interrogating our own biases and the structures of privilege that grades enable and reinforce.

## 3

# Why I Don't Grade

Not giving grades doesn't always feel like a radical pedagogy for me, because I've been doing it to different degrees for over 20 years. I've taught 100 sections of courses at a half-dozen institutions in a half-dozen disciplines. I've taught traditional students, nontraditional students, for credit, not for credit, online, in classrooms, as a tenure-track professor, as an adjunct, at small liberal arts colleges (SLACs), at a community college, and at research universities (R1s). But I have not always felt I could be publicly open about my approach to grading at the institutions where I've worked.

My ideas about grades and assessment have evolved over the years, as I've become a more confident teacher. But I am even more certain of what I instinctively knew when I taught my first class in 2001 as instructor of record: grades are the biggest and most insidious obstacle to education. And they're a thorn in the side of Critical Pedagogy. John Holt writes in *Instead of Education*, "Competitive schooling, grades, credentials seem to me the most authoritarian and dangerous of all the social inventions." Agency, dialogue, self-actualization, and social justice are not possible in a hierarchical system that pits teachers against students and encourages competition by ranking students against one another. Grades are currency for a capitalist system that reduces teaching and learning to a mere transaction. They are an institutional instrument of compliance that works exactly because grades have been so effectively naturalized. Grading is a massive coordinated effort to take humans out of the educational process.

**Grades are not good incentive.** They incentivize the wrong stuff: the product over the process, what the teacher thinks over what the student thinks.

**Grades are not good feedback.** They are both too simplistic, making something complex into something numerical (8/10, 85%), and too complicated, offering so many gradations as to be inscrutable (A, A-, A/A-, 92.4%, 9.5/10).

**Grades are not good markers of learning.** They too often communicate only a student's ability to follow instructions, not how much she has learned. A 4.0 or higher GPA might indicate excellence, but it might also indicate a student having to compromise their integrity for the sake of a grade.

**Grades encourage competitiveness over collaboration.** Supposed kindnesses, like grading on a curve or norming, actually increase competitiveness by pitting students (and sometimes teachers) against one another.

**Grades don't reflect the idiosyncratic, subjective, often emotional character of learning.**

Finally, **grades aren't fair.**

All of this demands exactly two pedagogical approaches:

1. Start by trusting students.
2. Realize "fairness" is not a good excuse for a lack of compassion.

My approach to assessment arises from these two principles. While I've experimented with many alternatives to traditional assessment, I have primarily relied on self-assessment, asking students to do the work of reflecting critically on their own learning. I turn in final grades at the end of the term, but those grades usually match the grades students have given themselves.

Amy Fast writes, "the saddest and most ironic practice in schools is how hard we try to measure how students are doing and how rarely we ever ask them." We have created increasingly elaborate assessment mechanisms, all while failing to recognize that students themselves are often the best experts in their own learning. Certainly metacognition, and the ability to self-assess, must be developed, but I see it as one of the most important skills we can teach in any educational environment.

I include the following statement about assessment in my syllabi:

> This course will focus on qualitative not quantitative assessment, something we'll discuss during the class, both with reference to your own work and the works we're studying. While you will get a final grade at the end of the term, I will not be grading individual assignments, but rather asking questions and making comments that engage your work rather than simply evaluate it. You will also be reflecting carefully on your own work and the work of your peers. The intention here is to help you focus on working in a more organic way, as opposed to working as you think you're expected to. If this process causes more anxiety than it alleviates, see me at any point to confer about your progress in the course to date. If you are worried about your grade, your best strategy should be to join the discussions, do the reading, and complete the assignments. **You should consider this course a "busy-work-free zone."** If an assignment does not feel productive, we can find ways to modify, remix, or repurpose the instructions.

It's important to note that an ungraded class does not mean grades don't influence the work that happens there. (My students are still graded in their other classes.) Grades are ubiquitous in our educational system to the point that new teachers don't feel they can safely explore alternative approaches to assessment. In my experience, new teachers are rarely told they have to grade, but grading is internalized as imperative nonetheless. And student expectations and anxiety can still swirl around grades even when they're taken mostly off the table.

Google Trends shows increased search volume around the term "grades" over the last 20 years. It also shows an increasingly furious pattern of search-behavior centered each year around the months of May and December, like a heartbeat beginning to race. Nervous attention turns to grades at specific times throughout the year, and that nervous attention is on the rise. This has been my anecdotal experience as well, as I've watched the increasing anxiety around grades become more and more palpable.

I find myself drowning in buzzwords.

*Learning Outcomes*

More and more, we are required to map our assignments, assessments, and curricula to learning outcomes. But I find it strange that teachers and institutions would predetermine outcomes before actual students even enroll for a course. I argue, instead, for emergent outcomes, ones that are cocreated by teachers and students and revised on the fly. Setting trajectories rather than mapping in advance the possible shapes for learning.

*Grade Inflation*

The problem is grades not inflation. And when institutions try to control for grade inflation, the results are disturbing, and maybe also unsurprising. Require teachers to give more B and C grades and they give more B and C grades disproportionately to black students (Nelson). We should be creating opportunities, not limiting possibilities for success. If all our students earn As, that should be a good thing. Why wouldn't it be our goal to have all students succeed or excel? Inflation presumes grades should function as currency and that the goal of education is to rank students against one another (rather than to help students learn). The best feedback I've ever gotten from a student, and something I've since tried to reflect more explicitly in my pedagogy: "Jesse's class was one of the hardest I've taken in my life; it was an easy 'A'." *Hard*, because the student was challenged in ways they wouldn't have otherwise been if I'd had harsh guidelines and an objective rubric; *easy*, because the assessment of their learning in the course never felt arbitrary or mysterious.

Having and encouraging high expectations and giving mostly good grades are not incompatible.

*Grade-grubbing*

If this phrase is still in your vocabulary, do a quick internet search for the words "grub" and "grubber," and I suspect you'll stop attributing these words to students. As educators we have helped build (or are complicit in) a system that creates a great deal of pressure around grades. We shouldn't blame (or worse, degrade) students for the failures of that system.

*Objectivity*

I don't think pure objectivity is a virtue if dialogue is what we're after in education. Human interaction is incredibly complex. Authentic feedback (and evaluation) means honoring subjectivity and requires that we show up as our full selves, both teachers and learners, to the work of education. Grades can't be normed if we recognize the complexity of learners and learning contexts. Bias can't be accounted for unless we acknowledge it.

*Rubrics*

Most rubrics I've seen are overly mechanistic and attempt to create objectivity and efficiency in evaluation by crashing on the rocks of bureaucracy. Learning and human interaction is sufficiently high resolution that a 5 × 5 grid, or even a 3 × 3 grid, usually fails to capture the complexity of learning or student work. And when rubrics are given in advance to students, they are likely to close down possibility by encouraging students to work toward a prescribed notion of excellence.

*Participation Grades*

Too many of our conventional practices work to reduce the complexity of learning to its detriment. Grading participation, for example, is an exercise in futility. Different humans engage in different ways at different times, and much of that engagement is effectively invisible to crude quantitative mechanisms. Most grading scales offer way too many demarcations to communicate clearly and way too few demarcations to reflect reality. They frustrate organic participation by foregrounding control. We can't participate authentically, can't engage in real dialogue, without first disrupting the power dynamics of grading.

*Grades as Motivators*

Alfie Kohn writes in "The Trouble with Rubrics," "Research shows three reliable effects when students are graded: They tend to think less deeply, avoid taking risks, and lose interest in the learning itself." Grades do motivate, but they don't motivate the kinds of peak experiences that can happen in a learning environment. Something like *have an epiphany, communicate an original thought, sit uncomfortably with your not knowing,* or b*uild something that's never been built before* can't be effectively motivated by a grade.

*Grading on a Curve*

In brief, grading on a curve pits students against each other, discourages collaboration, and privileges the students who our educational system has already privileged. In "How Do We Measure What Really Counts In The Classroom?," Cathy N. Davidson writes, "There is an extreme mismatch between what we value and how we count."

*Mastery*

I've long argued education should be about encouraging and rewarding not knowing more than knowing. When I give presentations on grading and assessment, I often get some variation of the question, *How would you want your doctor to have been graded?* My cheeky first answer is that I am most concerned with whether my doctor has read all the books of Virginia Woolf or Octavia Butler, because critical thinking is what will help them save my life when they encounter a situation they've never encountered before. I go on to say I would want a mixture of things assessed and a mixture of kinds of assessment, because the work of being a doctor (or engineer, sociologist, teacher, etc.) is sufficiently complex that any one system of measurement or indicator of supposed mastery will necessarily fail.

There are many alternatives to traditional assessment and ways to approach ungrading, which I'll explore further in a later chapter. However, I think it's important to withhold the mechanics of ungrading to a certain degree, because I agree with Alfie Kohn who writes, "When the how's of assessment preoccupy us, they tend to chase the why's back into the shadows" ("The Trouble With Rubrics").

Grades are not something we should have ever allowed to be naturalized. Assessment should be, by its nature, an open question.

*4*

# Learning is Not a Mechanism

When I first taught fully online, I encountered the horror that is the grade book inside most learning management systems (LMSs), which reduces students (often color coding them) into mere rows in a spreadsheet. On its surface, the LMS grade book does not seem all that functionally different from an analog grade book, which also reduces students to rows in a spreadsheet.

Digital pedagogy is not equivalent to teachers using digital tools. Rather, digital pedagogy demands that we think critically about our tools, demands that we reflect actively upon our own practice. I have little interest in teaching teachers or learners how to use the technologies they'll use in classrooms for the next three years. I am much more interested in working with teachers and learners to develop the literacies that will help them use and evaluate the educational tools they'll be using in ten or twenty years. Often, this means knowing when and how to put tools down, as much as it means knowing when and how to take them up.

Talk of teaching with technology is not altogether (or even close to nearly) new. Even well before John and Evelyn Dewey's 1915 book, *Schools of To-Morrow*, the development and dissemination of educational technology has had political, as well as practical, ramifications.

The large-format blackboard was first used in the U.S. in 1801. The vacuum tube-based computer was introduced in 1946. In the 1960s, Seymour Papert began teaching the Logo programming language to children. The first Learning Management System, PLATO (Program Logic for Automatic Teaching Operations), was developed in 1960. At the invent of each, there was fear, resistance, and the thoughtless slobber of over-enthusiasm. After the introduction of the Radio Lecture in the 1930s, Lloyd Allen Cook warned, "This mechanizes education and leaves the local teacher only the tasks of preparing for the broadcast and keeping order in the classroom." This sentence is not all that different from the ones we've read about artificial intelligence over the last year, or about the Massive Open Online Course (MOOC) over the last ten years, or about online learning over the last twenty five years. In the 19th Century, Emily Dickinson hinted at the mechanizing of education in her poem, "From all the Jails the Boys and Girls," where she equates schools with jails but ultimately determines, "That Prison doesn't keep."

Most learning management systems offer (or threaten) to automate a process that is, in fact, deeply personal. Assessment is reduced to a mark, and the complexity of human interaction within a learning environment is made machine readable. The LMS grade book makes grading more efficient, as though efficiency is something we ought to valorize in teaching and learning.

It seems easy, to far too many teachers, administrators, and LMS-makers, to imagine students work the way machines do — that they can be scored according to objective metrics and neatly compared to one another. Schools, and the systems we've invented to support them, condition us to believe that there are always others (objective experts or even algorithms) who can know better than us the value of our own work. I'm struck by the number of institutions that for all intents and purposes equate teaching with grading — that assume our job as teachers is to merely separate the wheat from the chaff. And I find myself truly confused when anyone suggests there is a way for us to do this kind of work objectively. For me, teaching and learning have always been (and will always be) deeply subjective.

bell hooks writes in *Teaching to Transgress* about her experience in graduate school, "nonconformity on our part was viewed with suspicion, as empty gestures of defiance aimed at masking inferiority or substandard work." One of the problems with learning management system grade books, often mapped to rubrics and outcomes, is that they assume students (and their experiences) are interchangeable. And they assume the same of teachers. The problem is that syllabi, lesson plans, and assignments can't be expected to work exactly the same with every set of students, with every teacher, or on every given day. Both teachers and learners must approach the classroom from a place of flexibility, willing to see the encounters, exchanges, interactions, and relationships that develop in a classroom as dynamic. Grades, and the (very bizarre) notion of their systematized objectivity, stand as an immediate affront to this kind of classroom.

Several years ago, I worked with a student that admitted to stopping doing the work for the current week, because she was distracted by — "lost within," to use her words — a subject from a previous week. My response was simple and encouraging, "sounds good, stay lost." There would have been no column sufficient for representing this exchange in a grade book, and this kind of exchange has been the rule more than the exception in my work as a teacher. The text in question, Mark Z. Danielewski's *House of Leaves*, is about exactly what the student described to me, going on a quest and getting lost. This is, for me, what learning looks like — not finishing assignments, not following directions, not dotting "i"s and crossing "t"s. It's a process of discovery that has no outcome fixed in advance. This kind of learning is about sitting (sometimes uncomfortably) with our not knowing. Grading inside a learning management system too often obscures, does not reveal, this process.

I used these systems for years, struggling to find ways to subvert their worst intentions, until I ultimately determined to simply say, "I would prefer not to."

If there is a better sort of mechanism that we need for the work of teaching, it is a machine, an algorithm, a platform tuned not for delivering and assessing content, but for helping all of us listen better to students. And, by "listen," I decidedly do not mean "surveil." The former implies an invitation to open dialogue, whereas the latter implies a hierarchical relationship through which learners are made into mere data points. My call, then, is for more emphasis on the tools that help us fully and genuinely inhabit digital environments, tools like ears, eyes, or fingers. My call is to stop attempting to distinguish so incessantly between online and on-ground learning, between the virtual and the face-to-face, between digital pedagogy and chalkboard pedagogy. Good digital pedagogy is just good pedagogy.

bell hooks writes, in *Teaching to Transgress*, "The first

paradigm that shaped my pedagogy was the idea that the classroom should be an exciting place, never boring." So, what kinds of tools can we find, build, or imagine that help make the work of learning "fun," as hooks advocates? Can we imagine assessment mechanisms that encourage discovery, ones not designed for assessing learning but designed for learning through assessment? When do we decide that a tool isn't working, and how can we work together to set it down en masse?

5

## Love and Other Data Assets

For years, I've led pedagogical development seminars for faculty at numerous institutions focused on topics like "higher education pedagogy," "digital knowledge," and "reimagining assessment." These have included staff, librarians, adjunct faculty, junior faculty, senior faculty, STEM faculty, humanities faculty, social sciences faculty, fine arts faculty, current students, recently graduated students, and more. We've discussed practical issues arising from our own teaching, discussed readings, met with special guests, and done microteaching (offering feedback on short lessons taught by participants).

I've guided these discussions and chosen many of the readings, but the topics have arisen organically, usually beginning with a group-brainstorm at our first session. At any one of these seminars, what we've done was more important than what we set out to do, and we've reflected regularly on how we did it and why. The syllabi for these seminars have ended up an eclectic "mixtape" including non-fiction, documentary films, even comics, and ranging from classics (John Dewey, bell hooks, Seymour Papert) to curiosities (Virginia Woolf, Henry David Thoreau) to more contemporary choices (Sara Goldrick-Rab, Ruha Benjamin, Cathy N. Davidson). Sometimes, there has been a clear path from one week's topics to the next, but more often the juxtapositions have been haphazard, as much about generating friction as about finding common theses.

There is very little time, support, or funding in higher education for this kind of reflective consideration of our work. Teaching is quite often something we do alone with very little direct preparation for the work. Conversations between and among faculty, librarians, instructional designers, and technologists are much rarer than they should be. The faculty/staff divide at many Institutions limits our ability to talk across structural barriers. And contingent, adjunct, or precarious educators are too often left out of these conversations altogether. Each year I facilitated these seminars at University of Mary Washington, for example, it was a struggle to include (and compensate) adjuncts, librarians, and staff. Spending faculty development funds on non-faculty, even non-faculty with teaching assignments, was discouraged by administrators. In fact, every year, funding was eliminated altogether for this project, and I had to advocate (with the support of previous participants) for it to be reinstated. Even as the funding for the seminar was eliminated again in early 2020, the annual bill for the learning management system contract went up. This kind of decision-making sent a message that the administration wanted technical support, not deep inquiry into the complicated work of teaching.

Educational technology is strangely situated at many institutions (usually somewhere vaguely between academics and IT), which further frustrates necessary conversations across the teaching/technology divide. And, quite often, for-profit ed-tech companies take advantage of this situation through predatory marketing tactics — pitching their tools to the most powerful, least knowledgeable folks at an institution. The majority of ed-tech is driven by the bureaucratic traditions of education more than the pedagogical ones.

In "Teaching as Possibility: A Light in Dark Times," Maxine Greene writes, "It is obvious enough that arguments for the values and possibilities of teaching acts (no matter how enlightened) within the presently existing system cannot be expressed through poetry, even as it is clear that the notion of 'teaching as possibility' cannot simply be asserted and left to do persuasive work." What Greene describes is a conundrum. For her, the space of the imagination, the habitus of poetry, is necessary to the work of education. But how do we reconcile the philosophies of John Dewey with the fact of the learning management system? How does the work of Maria Montessori sit without combusting alongside the increasingly aggressive marketing of remote and algorithmic proctoring tools? How do bell hook's words about self-actualization in the classroom not wither in a world of key-stroke monitoring and plagiarism-detection software? And how can we honestly approach Virginia Woolf's *A Room of One's Own* with students if we're complicit in the monetization of their educational data by for-profit companies?

These crises aren't existential, nor are my examples purely hypothetical. The technological tools we've widely adopted for education are increasingly out of step with what we say education is for. There's a serious problem in education if we assume dishonesty on the part of students while failing to acknowledge that for-profit tech companies like Turnitin or ProctorU might care about their bottom line more than they care about students.

During a 2019 investor conference, the (now former) CEO of Instructure (maker of the Canvas learning management system) bragged about their "second growth initiative focused on analytics, data science, and artificial intelligence," saying: "We have the most comprehensive database on the educational experience in the globe ... No one else has those data assets at their fingertips to be able to develop those algorithms and predictive models." What concerns me are two specific words that fell so easily off that CEO's tongue: "data assets." Teachers and students have long been called "users" and "customers" by educational technology companies, and this has had me uncomfortable enough, but reducing us and our work to "data assets" takes this a step further, exposing the role that for-profit companies and technologies play in the increasing precarity of education and educational labor. It's not a coincidence that more than 70% of university teachers are working off the tenure-track and nearly 1 in 2 students in the U.S. is food insecure, even as Turnitin claims their product is used by more than 30 million students at 15,000 institutions in 150 countries and the global learning management system market is expected to reach $28.1 billion by 2025.

As these bureaucratic technological systems become more ubiquitous, educators increasingly accept them as inevitable instead of pushing back when institutions invest more and more in machines (and algorithms) and less and less in teachers (and the work of teaching). The biggest issues for me arise when we adopt tools across an entire educational institution, discipline, or curriculum and give teachers and students no choice but to use them. A student's degree or grade shouldn't rest on whether they are willing to sacrifice their privacy or give their data to a for-profit corporation. And institutions shouldn't allow the worst of these tools, like plagiarism detection and remote proctoring solutions, to short-circuit our best pedagogical intentions by creating a culture of distrust in education.

Grades are a big reason institutions adopt surveillance technologies that actively encourage a culture of suspicion in education, technologies like algorithmic retention platforms, remote proctoring tools, plagiarism and AI detection software, etc. And the abuses of these tools is not distributed equally. In "Our Bodies Encoded: Algorithmic Test Proctoring in Higher Education," Shea Swauger writes, "Algorithmic test proctoring encodes ideal student bodies and behaviors and penalizes deviations from that ideal by marking them as suspicious."

There's a common end game for tech companies, especially ones that traffic in human data: create a large base of users, collect their data, monetize that data in ways that help assess its value, then leverage that valuation in an acquisition deal. An educational institution should be skeptical of those companies, not suspicious of its own students.

In "Digital Sanctuary: Protection and Refuge on the Web?," Amy Collier writes, "We in higher education need to seriously consider how we think about and handle student data, and we need to respectfully and empathetically acknowledge where our practices may cause harm." This work starts by talking openly with one another, and across institutional divides. Collier's call is for dialogue, not empty bureaucratic structures. We all need to work together to ask hard questions of our technologies: Does the tool educate students about IP and data privacy before collecting data? Can individual students opt out, no matter the university policy? Is there a single button students can click to remove all their data? If the company does monetize the data it has collected, whether permission was given or not, will the owners of that data be compensated?

Asking these questions is necessary when a tool is institutionally adopted, but smaller versions of these conversations should happen every time we consider pointing to a tool on an institutional Web page or require the use of a tool for a course assignment. "If higher education is to 'save the Web,'" Chris Gilliard writes in "Pedagogy and the Logic of Platforms," "we need to let students envision that something else is possible, and we need to enact those practices in classrooms. To do that, we need to understand 'consent' to mean more than 'click here if you agree to these terms.'" Our work as educators is not just to question ubiquitous practices, compulsory data collection, and algorithmic decision-making, but also to model what it looks like to think critically about the whens, whys, and hows of technology.

The learning management system isn't an accident. It exists for very particular historical, bureaucratic, institutional, and pedagogical reasons. The same is true of remote proctoring software, plagiarism detection services, and algorithmically-driven mobile apps for student retention. These tools are not neutral. In an interview with Tara Robertson (from the book *Feminists Among Us*), Chris Bourg offers, "Many people don't proclaim their agendas, but definitely have agendas, even if they are agendas about maintaining the status quo, and never get asked about how they handle people in their organization who don't agree with their agendas." Bourg argues for a feminist administrative practice of radical openness and transparency about our own agendas. The onus has to be on the tech companies themselves to educate "users" about data security and data monetization.

Ed-tech companies need to state clearly: "Here's what we're collecting, here's why we're collecting it, here's what what we hope to do with it, here's why it should matter to you." Far too many companies attempt to shift these responsibilities entirely onto educational institutions, when they should be shared by students, educators, institutions, and the ed-tech companies themselves. We all need to talk honestly about what tools are for, how they might shift culture, and who they could disadvantage. We need to actively resist marketing jargon that would have us believe our "culture of academic integrity begins with Turnitin," or that ProctorU "validates knowledge." And by "resist," I mean we should not adopt tools that conceal their monetization strategy or lie to us about their function.

My work in critical digital pedagogy begins with the presumption that there aren't easy solutions in education — that students and educators bring complex backgrounds, experiences, and contexts to the work — and that this work demands we "gather together a cacophony of voices." This means acknowledging fractious (and sometimes abusive) faculty/staff divides, drawing students into the work of building their own educational spaces, and creating much more inclusive conversations between technology companies and all "stakeholders," the human beings, who populate (and construct) a university, college, or other school.

In the description for my "digital knowledge" pedagogical development seminar, I write, "Putting the word 'digital' in front of 'knowledge' begs a whole host of questions: How do digital technologies change the ways we produce, disseminate and consume knowledge? Does social media indeed have a democratizing effect, as some have suggested? What inequities has it unearthed or enhanced? When we say 'digital knowledge,' how can we see knowledge as acting also upon the digital? What is the role for educators in helping construct new pathways into, out of, and around the digital?" One of the first things I encourage participants to read in these seminars is *Teaching to Transgress* by bell hooks. It is productive to hold her work, which has been foundational for my own pedagogy, up against investigations into the past, present, and future of educational technologies.

Henceforth, every time I hear the phrase "data assets" to describe students, educators, and their work, I'm going to recite in my brain (or aloud) these words from another book by hooks, *Teaching Critical Thinking*:

> It is the most militant, most radical intervention anyone can make to not only speak of love, but to engage in the practice of love. For love as the foundation of all social movements for self-determination is the only way we create a world that domination and dominator thinking cannot destroy.

And thinking on those words, I'll be reminded of this from Paulo Freire's *Pedagogy of the Oppressed*, "If I do not love the world if I do not love life if I do not love people I cannot enter into dialogue."

We are not data assets. And the work of dialogue depends on that. It begins when we:

- build a community of care

- ask genuine, open-ended questions
- wait for answers
- let conversation wander
- model what it looks like to be wrong and to acknowledge when we're wrong
- recognize that the right to speak isn't distributed equally
- make listening visible

From there, we can find tools and technologies that support the project of education, ones that allow us to own our data, delete it at will, and export it easily — tools that allow "users" (human faculty, staff, librarians, adjuncts, administrators, technologists, and students) to create our own spaces (and conversations) on and about the Web — tools with an architecture of radical openness, love, imagination, hard questions, possibility, and poetry.

# 6

## If bell hooks Made a Learning Management System

Radical openness isn't a bureaucratic gesture. It has to be rooted in a willingness to sit with discomfort. The learning management system is not a space built for discomfort.

Radical openness in education means recognizing the ways in which the work of teaching is a kind of activism. The learning management system is not a space built for activism.

Radical openness demands the classroom be a space for genuine relationships, at the expense of content, summative assessment, and so-called academic rigor. The learning management system is a space built to track and score students — to gather them into rows, arrange their work into columns, feeding them into a machine that spits out a grade on the other end. The LMS is designed to make grading students convenient for teachers — and designed to facilitate the systematic observation (and scoring) of teachers by administrators. These are not dialogues.

At OpenEd 2014, Sean Michael Morris and I offered a presentation titled, "If Freire Made a MOOC: Open Education and Critical Digital Pedagogy." As we've continued to consider the intersection between critical and digital pedagogies, we've wondered at a follow-up question, "if bell hooks made a learning management system." Our answers in turn: "she wouldn't" and, more importantly, "her learning environment is not our space to build." Given how ubiquitous these systems have become in education, I think the better question to wonder at is whether the words (and pedagogies) of bell hooks can help dismantle the need for learning management systems altogether.

In our work on Freire and the MOOC, Sean and I wrote, "Ceding authority is an active endeavor. Dichotomies of leaders and learners, teachers and students, are only helpful when they facilitate rather than frustrate dialogue, and when we acknowledge these roles are permeable, transparent, and flexible." Our learning management systems have been designed, marketed, deployed to do just the opposite. These are systems of control, systems structured for obedience, systems structured to assert authority over students, systems structured to center the instructor. For the same reason that we shouldn't presume to (even imaginatively) build the LMS for bell hooks, we should have never built these systems for students. We shouldn't pre-determine the shape of our students' learning environment before meeting the students. And I say "we" pointedly, because even if we aren't implicated in the code of the LMS, all of us in education are in some way implicated in its use.

Many of us rail against learning management systems, poke holes at their flawed pedagogies, and even cuss at the particularly egregious ones, but most of us do little to chip away at their market share. Because the learning management system is a red herring, a symptom of a much larger beast that has its teeth on education: the crude quantification of learning, the reduction of teaching to widgets and students to data points.

**Alternatives to the Learning Management System**

In 2012, I designed and launched a new hybrid degree program at a small liberal arts institution in Oregon. It was a digital humanities program, and I argued that since it was about the Web, the program should live on the Web, and not in Moodle, the institution's learning management system. I set up a multisite WordPress installation as a homegrown alternative to an LMS. For each online course, I added a site and worked with instructors to find themes and plugins appropriate to their pedagogies. Students built sites of their own and connected with each other across the network of sites and via a social media hashtag for each course. The whole thing was certainly more chaotic than what happens in a learning management system, but still more structured than the dynamic interaction in most of my on-ground classrooms.

When I left that institution, the program continued, but it retreated immediately back into Moodle. For two main reasons: Moodle made it more convenient to share and structure content, and Moodle had a grade book. The failure of the program was not that I didn't build a suitable alternative to the LMS, but that I didn't sufficiently convince the instructors why they should use it. Most teaching practice is unexamined, because teachers in higher education are rarely asked to think critically about pedagogy. They structure learning as though students are interchangeable. They expect content mastery. They demand compliance with course policies. They wield expertise like a weapon. They grade. Because many have never thought not to. They've never had a reason not to. Because the problem is not individual teachers. The problem is systemic. We build systems that reflect our collective values, and that is what LMS-makers have done.

The challenge for me when I configured that multisite installation was to reflect a different set of values. This was also the challenge when I oversaw the evolution of the Domain of One's Own project at University of Mary Washington — to reflect a different set of values. At UMW, the institution asked students to build their own sites on the Web, dynamic places for their learning to inhabit, where the work from one class might blur into another. But we can't expect that just building new systems will magically change our teaching practices or the cultures at our institutions. Pedagogical work in and around these new systems must continually poke and prod at their intentions, the assumptions we've baked into them. This work requires a tirelessness, a head permanently and inquisitively cocked to one side. This work requires awe and sometimes circumspection.

Who does the system serve? What data does it collect? Who profits? What hierarchies does it reinforce or disrupt? Who does it allow under the hood? What is its default configuration? What pedagogies does that configuration make possible? Does it make visible to students the chinks in its own armor? What are the risks to students and teachers in subverting the system?

In *Teaching to Transgress*, bell hooks writes,

*Undoing the Grade*

My commitment to engaged pedagogy is an expression of political activism. Given that our educational institutions are so deeply invested in a banking system, teachers are more rewarded when we do not teach against the grain. The choice to work against the grain, to challenge the status quo, often has negative consequences.

Teaching is always a risk. Learning is always a risk. But that risk is not distributed evenly. A gay male administrator experiences the classroom differently from a black teacher, a disabled staff member, or a female student. Even a system that invites subversiveness, like Domain of One's Own or the WordPress multisite I launched at Marylhurst University in Oregon, can't single-handedly dismantle the institutionalized hierarchies of education.

While I was at University of Mary Washington, I participated in a series of programmatic assessment conversations — aimed (in part) at considering the effectiveness of Domain of One's Own as a curricular tool. The discussion was invaluable and led, as I believe programmatic assessment should, to more questions than answers. During one part of the process, we looked at a handful of Web sites designed by students. As we worked through them, I quickly recognized that I could tell less about the individual students by looking at their sites and more about the assignment they had been given and how they were being graded. A year later, the next round of sites we reviewed showed different results, students genuinely engaged in the work of exploring their digital identity. But I continue to worry when I see students given the task of building a Web site as a kind of elaborate (and sometimes draconian) busy work. If we are to genuinely push back on the constraints of the learning managements system, our goal must be to help students think critically about their place on the Web, and a series of point and click tasks with instrumental outcomes is not helping them move in that direction. "Post once, reply twice" in a discussion forum doesn't create dialogue or intrinsic motivation, nor does "add these five elements to your course site in order to receive full credit."

Andrew Rikard writes, in "Do I Own My Domain if You Grade it?," "Until students see this domain as a space that rewards rigor and experimentation, it will not promote student agency." The best learning spaces should not fall into the cracks of formal assignments and assessment; rather, they should subvert and even defy attempts at schooliness. A domain of one's own, or a portfolio of any sort, at its most "academically rigorous," doesn't overtly betray its origin as a graded set of tasks assigned by a teacher. Andrew Rikard continues, "The domains project isn't revolutionary to the traditional classroom, but it is revolutionary to a classroom reimagined around public scholarship, student agency and experimentation." This is key. We don't need an alternative LMS. The LMS does its job just fine. We need pedagogical approaches that help make the LMS irrelevant. When students take learning into their own hands, they have no use for learning management systems.

**Radical Openness**

bell hooks means something very specific when she talks of Radical Openness, and so far the Open Education movement has failed to tread that particular water. Projects like Domain of One's Own have flirted at the edge of Critical Pedagogy, but giving out free Domains isn't exactly the revolution Paulo Freire, bell hooks, or Virginia Woolf had in mind. It falls on us to inhabit the space of the Web in a decidedly different way than education has inhabited the LMS, the MOOC, or the traditional physical classroom, for that matter.

To be radically open, online learning spaces can't be delivery devices for content. They can't be mechanisms for turning in assignments. They can't be a mere replacement for the LMS. We have to let our own pedagogies stumble as we find new footing in these spaces.

bell hooks writes in "Choosing the Margin as a Space of Radical Openness," "Spaces can be real and imagined. Spaces can tell stories and unfold histories. Spaces can be interrupted, appropriated, and transformed through artistic and literary practice." We have to be willing to let new stories be told in education and to let students be the authors and co-authors of those stories. This means leaving policies, rubrics, grades, assignments, and other bureaucratic minutia at the door. Along with static content, learning objects, and mere resources. Everything that students have no hand in creating. What if dialogue were the stuff of open learning and not content? Radical openness means asking hard questions and having hard questions asked always of us.

hooks continues, "for me this place of radical openness is a margin — a profound edge. Locating oneself there is difficult yet necessary. It is not a 'safe' place. One is always at risk. One needs a community of resistance."

For hooks, the risks we take are personal, professional, political. When she says that "radical openness is a margin," she suggests it is a place of uncertainty, a place of friction, a place of critical thinking. This is not an open pedagogy neatly defined and delimited.

Audrey Watters writes in "From 'Open' to Justice, "We act — at our peril — as if 'open' is politically neutral, let alone politically good or progressive. Indeed, we sometimes use the word to stand in place of a politics of participatory democracy." When we use a word like "open," or ones like "agency" and "identity," these should not be just empty signifiers.

Supporting student agency means advocating for students as they make choices about their own work — what, when, and also *whether*. When we acknowledge students make choices, we must also prepare for the possibility that they'll say "no" — that they'll hack our assignments — that they'll choose their own paths, rather than the ones we set out for them. Sometimes, their work, their thinking, their process won't be visible to us. As a teacher, how can I grade work I don't see, or even work that doesn't exist, because a student has discarded it as part of their process?

**Grades Are a Technology**

Grades motivate, in at least some small way, every tool developed by edtech software and hardware engineers. In too many of our institutional and technological systems, every road leads back to the grade book.

As Peter Elbow writes, "Grading tends to undermine the climate for teaching and learning. Once we start grading their work, students are tempted to study or work for the grade rather than for learning" ("Grading Student Writing").

Ranking. Norming. Objectivity. Uniformity.

Measurement. Outcomes. Quality. Data. Performance. Metrics. Scores. Excellence. Mastery.

Over the last 20 years, I've watched the LMS proliferate into all the institutions where I've worked. Even teachers that don't use the learning management system for its other decidedly more pleasurable uses have made its grade book more and more central to the learning experience for students. To the point that, when I've chosen not to use the institutionally adopted LMS, students sometimes ask after the LMS in its absence. Not because the LMS has any particularly useful magic, but because we've come to expect it — to be comforted by the inevitability of its use. When a grade appears there, we feel a sense of completion, acknowledgment. A reassurance of our place in the education hierarchy, whether teacher or student. In *Now You See It*, Cathy Davidson calls the grade book a "prop," the "symbol of pedagogical power."

According to marketing statements on their public Web sites, Angel's "automated agents save time," Blackboard facilitates teacher-student "interaction" by "calculating grades," and Canvas calls its tool "speed grader." The problem is not just the fact of grades but the fetishization of them. There is no air for student agency to breathe in a system of incessant grading, ranking, and scoring.

Can we find increasingly creative ways to scaffold out of a grade book, and not into one?

## Undoing the Grade

In "Civil Disobedience," Henry David Thoreau writes, "Let your life be a counter-friction to stop the machine." And, "if it is of such a nature that it requires you to be the agent of injustice to another, then I say, break the law."

If I want students to feel empowered and free to do organic and genuine work on the Web, then I need to allow myself room to be a genuine reader of that work. Which means approaching that work as a reader would. If I want students to feel empowered and free to collaborate both within and beyond the class, then I need to also allow myself to be their collaborator. There is no room for grading students inside these relationships.

Usually when I talk of not grading, I do so with a caveat, and I point toward approaches that offer a middle ground. But I want to argue here that there really is no middle ground with a project like Domain of One's Own. Put simply, no, you don't own your domain if I grade it.

For all kinds of reasons, I'd argue that grading public work that students do on the Web, by any of our conventional academic metrics, undermines the work.

And as Martha Burtis has said, "there is still so much work we have to do." Work reimagining what learning and teaching can look like on the Web. More labor and even more heart.

# 7

# Grades are Dehumanizing: Ungrading is No Simple Solution

Grades are not a good measure of learning, they inhibit intrinsic motivation, and they create a competitive environment between students and hostile relationships between students and teachers. We can't entirely and immediately remove grades, because they are hard-coded into our educational systems, but teachers can (and should) furiously raise our collective eyebrows at grades. And we should do this work together with students.

For years when I started teaching, I'd say, "I don't grade," but that wasn't exactly true. While the students I work with self-evaluate, analyzing their own learning, I still turn in grades at the end of a term – once bubbling in circles on a Scantron sheet, now filling out a series of increasingly (and needlessly) complicated online forms. From the start, that final moment of crude measurement felt out of sync with the rest of my teaching. It still does.

Why has so much of our educational system privileged that final moment of measurement?

I'm a bit unsettled by the word "ungrading," even as I've helped frame the term, because it feels like a Zeitgeist, a fleeting moment in time in which the thinking about grades is shifting, away from crude quantification and toward an equally simplified notion that grades can just as easily disappear into the ether from which they came. However, grades have a history, and I've argued they're a "technology."

There is nothing ideologically neutral about grades, and there is nothing ideologically neutral about the idea that we can neat and tidily do away with grades. We can't simply take away grades without re-examining all of our pedagogical approaches, and this work looks different for each teacher, in each context, and with each group of students.

Most students were born into a system of crude quantification. I don't say "born into" flippantly. I have a 6-year-old, and I've watched her growth quantified in discrete ways since the day she was born. She's adopted, Black, and has two gay dads, so her "development" has always been a subject of peculiar discussion. She's had wonderful doctors, who see and engage her as the full (and rowdy) human that she is, but she is also regularly reduced to a data point, plotted upon a chart pre-determined before she came into the world. Assumptions are made about her because she's Black, because she's adopted, because she's a girl, because she has two dads. But the data already being collected about her has little to do with the full and lovely human being my daughter actually is in the world.

In a *Time* magazine article, "All Teachers Should Be Trained to Overcome Their Hidden Biases," Soraya Chemaly gathers and reflects upon data about how girls (and girls of color, in particular) encounter their education. In that piece, she cites a study showing black girls are twelve times more likely than their white counterparts to be suspended. While Black children make up less than 20% of preschoolers, they make up more than half of out-of-school suspensions. Each time I read or share this data I find myself shocked, wondering at when and how a preschooler would or could find themselves suspended. My shock, though, is a point of privilege. I can't fathom being suspended from preschool, because I showed up for preschool in a white, male, not-yet-recognizably queer body, and my disability is mostly invisible (or masked). My experience of school was different from the experience of my BIPOC classmates, different from the experience my daughter will have.

Every bit of who are students have been, and the material circumstances they face, influences how they do (and can) engage.

> "Today's college students are the most overburdened and undersupported in American history. More than one in four have a child, almost three in four are employed, and more than half receive Pell Grants but are left far short of the funds required to pay for college." ~ Sara Goldrick-Rab and Jesse Stommel, "Teaching the Students We Have Not the Students We Wish We Had"

195,000 college students responded to the Hope Center's 2020 #RealCollege Survey. Nearly 3 in 5 experienced basic needs insecurity. Just over one-third of students experienced moderate to severe depression.

Students from marginalized groups are more likely to experience basic needs insecurity. 70% of Black students, 75% of Indigenous students, and 65% of LGBTQ students experienced basic needs insecurity. Female students were seven percentage points more likely than male students to experience basic needs insecurity. (Hope Center 2020 #RealCollege survey)

This is the world "ungrading" lives within, and it's not a world where easy answers, or universalized best practices, are useful — or possible. A student in the class we're "ungrading" might be the very same student who was suspended from preschool because she was a girl of color, or they might be dealing with food insecurity. This is why I've written with Sara Goldrick-Rab that we need to "teach the students we have, not the students we wish we had."

Most of our assessment mechanisms in higher education don't assess what our institutions say they value most. Glancing at even just a few college and university mission statements, I see none of the following:

- We pit students and teachers against one another
- We rank students in fiercely competitive ways.
- We measure output with little concern for the learning process.
- We demean student work by crudely quantifying it.
- We start from a place of deep suspicion of students.
- We assess in ways that reinforce bias against marginalized students.

And, yet, these are what far too many of our systems and technologies valorize.

I've written previously about the ways our technologies have attempted to "manage" the complexity of grades (and assessment). So much of edtech — learning management systems, remote proctoring, plagiarism detection software

— does little more than surveil students, reducing them to codified bits, readable by an algorithm, or able to be parsed at a glance in a column of 75 other students. So few of these digital tools seem to deeply understand the work of teaching, which is necessarily about humans working together with other humans. Spreadsheets do little to help this work; they're a distraction at best, an abuse at worst.

When our work moves online, as it did for so many of our institutions over the last several years, inequities and biases are exacerbated. We dehumanize students when we reduce them to squares in a videoconferencing platform (algorithmically arranged into a clear hierarchy) or when we use platforms (like the LMS) that resist experimentation, improvisation, and engagement. The relationship between students and teachers suffers when our systems and policies reinforce hierarchies, encode biases, and encourage policing.

Grades are anathema to the presumption of the humanity of students, support for their basic needs, and engaging them as full participants in their own education. Invigilated exams won't ensure integrity. Plagiarism detection tech won't unseat online paper mills. Incessant surveillance won't help us listen better for the voices of students asking for help. All of our efforts would be better served by three simple words, "I trust you."

## 8

# How to Ungrade

"I can't think of a more meaningless, superficial, cynical way to evaluate learning." ~ Cathy N. Davidson

The work of teaching shouldn't be reduced to the mechanical act of grading or marking. Our talk of grading shouldn't be reduced to our complaining about the continuing necessity of it.

If you're a teacher and you hate grading, stop doing so much of it.

Across education, we've normalized absurd levels of grading, test-taking, and standardized assessment. As I was preparing to write this piece, I looked through Web pages offering advice on grading at a dozen higher education institutions (most from teaching and learning centers). What I noticed is how so much of the language around grading emphasizes efficiency over the needs of individual learners. Nods to fairness are too often made for the sake of defensibility rather than equity. One site, for example, encourages "discussing grades with students" as a way toward making those grades "less likely to be contested." The work of grading is too often framed less in terms of encouraging learning and more as a way of ranking students against one another. Another site argues that "grades should be monotonic: within any pair of students, the student with better performance should not be given a lower grade." Others have headings like "grading as a fair teaching tool," "limit grading time," "responding to grade challenges," "maintaining your sanity," "easing the pain," and "making grading more efficient." What disturbs me is how effortlessly and casually this language rolls off Education's collective tongue. And I'm even more disturbed by how many otherwise productive pedagogical conversations get sidetracked by the bureaucratic dimensions of grades.

The page from the Berkeley Graduate Division offering "Tips on Grading Efficiently," for example, is pretty standard fare. The very first bit of advice on grading for new graduate student instructors raises more anxiety around grades than it alleviates. And at the same time, as is all too common, grading is something new teachers are encouraged to spend as little time on as possible: "Too often, time spent grading takes away from time spent doing your own coursework or research."

Without much critical examination, teachers accept that they have to grade, students accept that they have to be graded, students are made to feel like they should care a great deal about grades, and teachers are told they shouldn't spend much time thinking about the why, when, and whether of grades. Obedience to a system of crude ranking is made to feel altruistic, because it is supposedly fair, saves time, and helps prepare students for the horrors of the "real world." Conscientious objection seems increasingly impossible.

When I talk about why I don't grade, I often hear back some version of, *but I have to grade … because I'm an adjunct … because my institution requires it … because grading is necessary in my discipline … because wouldn't you want your heart surgeon to have been graded?* The need to navigate institutional (and disciplinary) pressures is real, but I would argue teachers grade in many more situations than grading is useful or is required by institutions. When I was a "road warrior adjunct," teaching up to nine courses at four institutions, how I taught and how I talked about my pedagogy were different from one institution to the next. I had to balance my own approach with the specific requirements at each institution. But I can also say that none of the institutions where I've worked has entirely dictated how I had to approach assessment — at every single one there was sufficient wiggle room for some amount of experimentation.

Peter Elbow writes in "Ranking, Evaluating, Liking: Sorting Out Three Forms of Judgement," "Let's do as little ranking and grading as we can. They are never fair and they undermine learning and teaching." I start almost every talk I give by saying that "I don't proselytize about pedagogy." I believe pedagogy is personal and idiosyncratic. My approach won't necessarily work in each classroom, at every institution, for all teachers, with every group of students. My hope in this chapter and in this book is to challenge stock assumptions, describe what has worked for me, and explore alternatives that just might work for others.

**How I Don't Grade**

My specific approach has evolved over the years. Currently, I have students write several self-reflections throughout the term. I have moved away from calling these "self-evaluations," because I want to de-emphasize the quantitative component of this work. Students do give themselves grades, but the primary goal is to help students develop their ability to do this kind of metacognitive work. Self-evaluation and metacognition are not easy, even for me, so I give students space to figure out how to do this work as they go.

I am often asked if (and how) I deal with student pushback in an ungraded class. Of course, being asked to do this work is a challenge. For as much anxiety as grades can create, being graded is something most of us find comfortable. Students are increasingly conditioned to work within a system that emphasizes objective measures of performance and quantitative assessment. It's important to acknowledge that these systems have been (in some cases intentionally) crafted to privilege certain kinds of students. It's also important to acknowledge that, in lieu of these systems, there are tacit expectations that still favor already privileged students. Students who are female, Black, Brown, Indigenous, disabled, neurodivergent, queer, etc. face overt and systemic oppression whether expectations are explicit or implicit. Soraya Chemaly writes, "Training teachers to understand bias will not eliminate it, but it could create an institutional environment in which it is clear that understanding bias and its effects is critically important."

Whether we're grading or not grading, we need to think critically (and talk openly with students) about our approach, assumptions, tacit expectations, actual expectations, etc. But we don't need to grade just because students will be graded elsewhere, because we shouldn't prepare students for a world of potential oppression by oppressing them.

Over many years, I've found that not grading begins a set of necessary conversations among my colleagues, between me and students, and among students in my classes. What students have written to me in self-reflections and self-evaluations is profoundly different from the kinds of interactions we would have in a purely transactional system. Their reflections, and my responses to them, become a space of dialogue, not just about the course, but about their learning and about how learning happens. Not every interaction rises to that level but many do. What happens with every single student is that any assumption I might make about them is squashed by what they write about themselves and their work. My view of students as complex and deeply committed to their education is fueled by the tens of thousands of self-reflection letters I've read over my career.

At the end of the term, every institution where I've worked has required me to submit a final grade for students. So, I ask the students to grade themselves. I wish I didn't have to do this. I wish the conversation I had with students could focus purely on authentic assessment, process, and formative feedback. But I have found that asking students to give themselves a grade also makes the why and how of grades a valuable subject of the conversations we have — valuable because they will go on to be graded in other courses and thinking critically about how and why grading happens helps that become more productive for them.

I'm frequently asked what I do when I disagree with a grade a student gives themselves. I don't intend my answer to be flip, but I say some version of, "it isn't really my place to worry at length about that." If I'm going to give the responsibility of grading over to students, I have to let go of my attachment to what I might perceive as the "accuracy" of that process. Instead, I give feedback, and the need for objectivity or accuracy gives way to a conversation — one that is necessarily emergent and subjective. Students give themselves the full range of grades in my classes. I rarely change the grades students give themselves, and almost always to raise grades, with addressing internalized bias as the primary reason I intervene. The most common change I've made is from an A- to an A for students who offer no good reason other than modesty for giving themselves the A- grade. I have observed a distinct gender imbalance in this, with women students much more likely to give themselves an A-.

**Alternative Approaches to Assessment**

Grading and assessment are two distinct things, and

spending less time on grading does not necessarily mean spending less time on assessment. Assessment is inevitable, constantly happening whether we're intentional about it or not. Ungrading asks us to question our assumptions about what assessment looks like, how we do it, and who it is for. Ungrading works best when teachers feel they can fully own their pedagogical approaches (which requires that administrators and institutions defend the academic freedom of teachers, especially adjuncts). There are lots of different possible paths toward ungrading, and smaller experiments can be just as fruitful as larger ones.

*Grade Free Zones*

Sometimes it's hard to imagine diving right into the deep end of removing grades, so you might consider having the first third of the term be ungraded, a sandbox for students to experiment inside before moving on to the more formal activities of a course. Or decide to grade only a few major assignments.

*Self-assessment*

I've already talked at length about how I use self-assessment. What I'll add is that this work is both part of my approach to the problem of grades and also a pedagogical end in and of itself. Ann Berthoff writes in "Dialectical Notebooks and the Audit of Meaning,"

"Learning to look carefully, to see what you're looking at, is perennially acclaimed as the essential skill for both artist and scientist." Metacognition is a practical skill that cuts across disciplines. In addition to reflecting on our own individual work, I would add that we — teachers and students — should evaluate our collective work together, the class itself.

*Process Letters*

If you're only grading a few assignments, you may not feel like you have enough information to determine a final grade at the end of a course. I have students write process letters, describing their learning and how their work evolves over the term. These work particularly well for creative and digital work that might otherwise seem inscrutable within traditional grading and feedback systems. A process letter can be text, including (or pointing to) representative examples of work students don't otherwise turn in. You might also ask students to take pictures of their work as it evolves, add voice-over to a screencast, or document their learning via film (a sort of behind-the-scenes reel for the class).

*Minimal Grading*

In "Grading Student Writing: Making It Simpler, Fairer, Clearer," Peter Elbow describes what he calls "minimal grading," using a simple grading scale instead of giving students bizarre grades like 97%, 18/20, or A–/B+. Scales with too many gradations make it difficult for teachers to determine grades and even more difficult for students to interpret them. The only legible difference between 94% and 97% is that 97% is higher than 94%, so a percentile scale is effective at ranking students against one another but not very effective at conveying clear information about performance. Elbow recommends scales with fewer gradations: turned in (one gradation), pass/fail (two gradations), strong/satisfactory/weak (three gradations). He also describes a "zero scale," in which some work is assigned but not collected at all. This frees teachers from feeling they have to respond to, evaluate, or even read every bit of work students do. And this last, moving away from student work as a thing to be collected, can help build intrinsic motivation to do the work of a course.

*Authentic Assessment*

In my film production courses, I often ask students to organize a film festival or premiere in order to share their work for the class. These usually include talk-backs with the audience. Increasingly, I don't ask students to turn any assignments into me (aside from their self-reflections). The community of the class (including me but not just me) becomes their audience. I allow myself space to be one member of that community, a genuine reader of student work. In a service learning course, this community expands even further beyond the boundaries of the class. In short, how can we create reasons more meaningful than points for students to do the work of a course?

*Contract Grading*

Grading contracts convey expectations about what is required for each potential grade. In "A Grade-Less Writing Course That Focuses on Labor and Assessing," Asao B. Inoue argues for "calculating course grades by labor completed and dispensing almost completely with judgments of quality." Contract grading pushes against the relegating of people into categories ("A student," "B student,") by keeping the focus on the work. Contract grading can be humane in a way that standardized teacher-centered rubrics usually are not. Contracts do run the risk of centering grades even more than traditional grading, but at their best, the negotiating around the contract becomes a way for students to collectively worry the edges of grading as a system.

*Portfolios*

Increasingly, many corporate e-portfolio platforms are walled gardens, giving students a regimented way of gathering together their work for the purposes of assessment. I prefer more authentic portfolios that have use value beyond the needs of individual, course, programmatic, or institutional assessment. Having students build personal or professional sites on the Web, for example, can help them craft a digital identity that exists outside (but also in conversation with) their coursework. The key is to use a portfolio not as a mere receptacle for assignments but as a metacognitive space, one with immediate practical value (as a way for students to share their work with potential collaborators, employers, graduate schools, etc.).

*Peer-assessment*

Peer-assessment can be formal (having students evaluate each other's work) or informal (having students actively engage each other's work). It can be particularly useful when students work in large groups. I frequently ask students to work on projects that have an entire class (of twenty-five or more) collaborating. When I do this, I ask every student to write a process letter that addresses their own contributions as well as the functionality and dynamic of the team they're working with. I do not ask students to grade each other. With large-group projects, it is hard for me to see what and how each student contributes, but peer-assessment helps me get a view into a process I might not otherwise be able to see. If it is a project students work on across the entire term, asking students to write process letters multiple times also allows me to get the information I need to step in and help when and where I'm needed.

*Student-made Rubrics*

I'll be honest. I don't love rubrics. Alfie Kohn, in "The Trouble with Rubrics," describes them as an "attempt to deny the subjectivity of human judgment." Rubrics are often recommended as a way to make standards for evaluation transparent, but rubrics have never helped me make sense of grading or being graded. Learning is just too complex to fit into neat and tidy little boxes. Peter Elbow encourages making rubrics plainer and more direct, a 3 × 3 or smaller grid. The rubrics I find most exciting are ones crafted with students — so that the making of the rubric becomes an act of learning itself rather than a device (or set of assumptions) created in advance of students arriving to a course.

Each of these alternative approaches can work on their own or in combination. With classes of twenty-five or three hundred. (You aren't going to write an individual letter responding to every student self-evaluation in a class of three hundred, but you can write a letter to the whole class, talking about the trends you notice and suggestions for moving forward.) Ultimately any assessment strategy demands us to adapt, in the moment, as we encounter each new group of students. This attention to context, our own and our students', is what critical pedagogy calls for.

Grades are a morass education has fallen into that frustrates our ability to focus on student learning. But, as long as grades remain ubiquitous in education, can we be more creative in how we approach them? At the very least, our talk of grading shouldn't be reduced to our complaining about its continuing necessity.

# 9

# Compassionate Grading Policies

The phrase "compassionate grading policies" is an oxymoron.

Early in 2020, educational institutions across the U.S. (and around the world) were having discussions about how to grade in the midst of a pandemic, something I heard repeatedly described as a "compassionate grading policy." For at least a single term, many institutions offered some version of a pass/fail approach to grading, but the majority of these initiatives failed to adequately inspect grades as a system. From the start, I wondered why more institutions hadn't been talking about "compassionate grading" prior to the pandemic. And as institutions have begun "pivoting" back to "business as usual," I find myself wondering why all these supposedly compassionate policies wouldn't simply continue. Is cruelty a necessary precondition for grades?

When the institution where I taught in early 2020 began its own decision-making process about shifting to some variation of a pass/fail system, input from faculty was collected in a Google document. The text produced was 13 single-spaced pages with just under 7000 words. The most common word is "students," which appears 138 times. The word "GPA" appears 20 times. The word "struggling" appears 9 times. The word "stress" appears 8 times.

I wrote in that document:

> I would encourage us to make sure to center student voices as much as possible in this discussion. Many of us are talking to students and trying hard to help, but the students most likely to be in close communication with us are the students who are best able to cope with this situation. Many other students are overwhelmed and have gone quiet. Those are most likely the students already marginalized to begin with, queer students, disabled students, first generation students, Black students, students already experiencing basic needs insecurity, etc. In the last two weeks, I've heard from students who are food insecure, LGBTQ students struggling to find a support system, students who have lost their jobs, students afraid they might lose scholarships, students with intense anxiety. For those students, "business as usual" is not possible, and it's not even possible to fake it.

Students were not initially asked to contribute in any meaningful way to the decision-making process around grades at my institution, so the students quickly assembled their own Google document, arguing that the institution and its faculty were "clearly lacking student input on this critical decision." The student document grew to 48 single-spaced pages with almost 26,000 words. The most common word in that document is also "students," appearing 327 times. The word "health" appears 50 times. "Stress" appears 64 times. "Struggle" appears 52 times. "Anxiety" appears 18 times. "Access" appears 26 times. And "worry" appears 30 times. At least 3 students write in the document about being food insecure, 2 reference being housing insecure, and 11 write about their own disability or concern for other students with disabilities. The word "GPA" appears 77 times in that student feedback document, which I still find heartbreaking. In March 2020, worry about how a compassionate (in this case, pass/fail) grading policy would affect their GPAs was at the top of students' minds. Students were also worried about whether pass/fail grades would be accepted for transfer or as prerequisites for medical school.

If an institution continued grading during the pandemic, here's what all those grades were measuring: how well students and teachers "pivoted" to working online, whether students had necessary access to course materials and meetings, whether they had support at home, whether they had homes from which to "shelter in place," and how capable students were of "performing" in a crisis. What all those grades mostly weren't measuring: student learning, engagement, and/or content knowledge. But this is not unique to grading in the midst of a pandemic. Nor was my former institution's decision to not include students in a conversation about a compassionate grading policy. The biggest cruelty of grades as a system is that they frustrate the already tenuous relationships between students and teachers, and between teachers and their institutions.

I have never been a fan of "best practices," because the notion presumes there is one universal set of practices that will work for every teacher, at every school, with every student. Instead, I describe "good-for-some-people-in-some-contexts practices." One of those I've offered most frequently over the last two years is for teachers to reassure students that a rug won't get pulled out from under them. I suggest doing this clearly, directly, and multiple times. And, then, teachers (and institutions) need to actually not pull rugs out from under students.

Compassionate grading in a pandemic (or anytime) isn't just about rewriting policies. It has to be about engaging students more fully and critically in conversations about their own education. At the start of the first pandemic lockdown, I wrote to all the students in my classes,

> I'm here to support you however I can. Take care of yourself and your family first. Our class should not be your priority. Everything about this class is flexible. Whatever happens, we will work it out.

A few months later, I wrote a piece for *Academe* about my own experience of the pandemic, "Care is a Practice; Care is Pedagogical." I wrote about my husband being laid off from his job, about our cat dying, about my mom's brain hemorrhage, about telling our 3-year-old (now 6-year-old) that her grandma might die. We can't be afraid to have frank conversations with students about our working conditions and their learning conditions.

We do need to restructure our policies. However, as we find new ways to reach out to students asking for help, and not just in the midst of a pandemic, we also need new (more direct, more honest) ways to draw students into conversation about our pedagogies, not just the what of teaching, but the how and why.

Ultimately, grading and assessment can't be "compassionate," unless it's work we do with students rather than something that happens to them.

## How I'm Grading in the Midst of a Pandemic

I've written over the years about my various approaches to ungrading. I've written about why I don't grade, how I ungrade, shared answers to frequently asked questions, assembled a bibliography, and more. Meanwhile, the world has changed, education has changed. I've continued to question my own practices. In 2022, I publicly shared excerpts from the syllabus I was designing for my courses. In one social media thread, I wrote,

> As a teacher, my job is to advocate for students — to stand in the gap between students and institutional policies that do harm. Of course, I am also precarious, and so I am left to rely on administrators to stand in the gap for me.

In another thread, I shared the basic needs and accessibility statements from my syllabus, in which I write,

> What's most important to me is that you feel able to show up fully to our work together. I'm human first. Students are human first.

The last bit of my syllabus that I revised was the "Grades and Assessment" section. And it was a struggle to find the words to clearly express my approach. Even after so many years of not putting grades on student work, I still internalize the tacit assumptions and expectations of our educational institutions. I wonder if students will just stop doing the work if I don't grade them. (They haven't.) I wonder if students will stop showing up if I don't give marks for attendance. (They don't.) I worry I'm not actually doing the work of teaching if I'm not grading. (I am.) I worry I might be fired, or reprimanded, if I push too hard on the system or cultural environment in which I work. (I haven't been.) As much as I have resisted, these voices in my head still kept me from boldly writing the "compassionate grading policy" I've always felt compelled to write.

I've previously written, "grades are a thorn in the side of Critical Pedagogy." I've written, "grades frustrate our ability to focus on student learning." And I've written, "Grades are not a good measure of learning, they inhibit intrinsic motivation, and they create a competitive environment between students and hostile relationships between students and teachers."

Ungrading isn't enough.

As I've previously defined it, "'Ungrading' means raising an eyebrow at grades as a systemic practice, distinct from simply 'not grading.' The word is a present participle, an ongoing process, not a static set of practices." And this work has to continue, because whether and how we grade can't instantly and altogether change the larger culture of grades that permeates our educational institutions. But given the unequivocal harm of grades, I am working harder to mitigate that harm and wanting (needing in this moment) to get even closer to "not grading" — and also looking toward a time when I won't even need to have students grade themselves (which has been my practice for much of my career).

Clutching onto overly bureaucratic policies for grading (or attendance) sends a clear message to students that the complexities of their lives don't matter.

Here is how the statement in my syllabus about grades has evolved. It begins with a quote from Alfie Kohn's "The Case Against Grades":

> Extrinsic motivation, which includes a desire to get better grades, is not only different from, but often undermines, intrinsic motivation, a desire to learn for its own sake.

And then:

> Everyone who participates in our course community and completes their self-reflections will get an 'A.' Instead of your grade, here's what I want you to focus on:
> 
> Actively engage in the work of the course. Writing is ultimately what this course is about, but there will be lots of different ways for each of us to engage.
> 
> Determine what participation in our community looks like for you – online, in-person, synchronously, asynchronously, on Discord, in our physical classroom, wherever you can best contribute and learn. Listening and reflecting can be just as important as speaking and

questioning. Writing is not an independent exercise, so I encourage you to focus a good amount of your energy on helping your peers, reading their work, championing their accomplishments, and offering feedback that pushes them in their own writing process.

Reflect on your own work. This course is about process, not product, and so writing about our own writing is the most important work we'll do.

I will not be grading individual assignments, but rather asking questions and making comments that engage your work rather than simply evaluate it. The intention is to help you focus on working in a more organic way, as opposed to working as you think you're expected to. If this process causes more anxiety than it alleviates, see me at any point to confer about your work in the course to date.

In a section at the start of the syllabus called, "What We'll Do and How We'll Do It," I've written this:

> Our world is increasingly complex, and so we can't know exactly what shape this course will take over the next several months. Not all of us are encountering this moment in the same ways, so each of us will have to make decisions about how we can engage.

The phrase "I trust you" appears multiple times throughout this revision of my syllabus. Ultimately, I think trust is the thing that should drive our grading policies, even more than compassion.

## 10

# Toward a Co-intentional Approach to Assessment

The work of ungrading is focused on asking critical questions about assessment with the goal of dismantling a dysfunctional system that does harm to students, and also teachers. In "When We Talk About Grades, We Are Talking About People," Sean Michael Morris writes, "Deciding to ungrade has to come from somewhere, has to do more than ring a bell, it has to have pedagogical purpose, and to be part of a larger picture of how and why we teach." The books I was reading when I first learned to teach, when I began to devise my own approaches to assessment, were bell hooks's *Teaching to Transgress* and Paulo Freire's *Pedagogy of the Oppressed*. Their words on

Critical Pedagogy echo inside my own thinking about grades.

Critical Pedagogy is focused on helping students become "readers of their world," in the words of Paulo Freire. bell hooks extends this in her writing about "continual self-evaluation." In *Teaching to Transgress*, she writes, "To teach in a manner that respects and cares for the souls of our students is essential if we are to provide the necessary conditions where learning can most deeply and intimately begin." This means acknowledging the full and complex humanity of students and also working to mitigate the harm done by systems that too often fail to see students and teachers as full humans.

A meta-analysis from Malouff and Thorsteinsson, which included data from 20 studies of 1,935 graders, found that "bias can occur in subjective grading when graders are aware of irrelevant information about the students." What they call "irrelevant information" included sex, race, disability, physical attractiveness, or knowledge of prior performance. The authors ultimately suggest "blind grading," the practice of grading with no identifying information about students beyond the work being assessed. But I'd argue that race, gender, and ability do not constitute "irrelevant information." We can't counter bias by ignoring it. Who students are is exactly relevant, and their specific contexts need to be accounted for in our approach to assessment.

Sharma and Carr found that "food insecurity is a significant factor in determining the average Math-SAT score. An increase in food insecurity lowers the students' Math-SAT scores." And Cotti, et. al. found that students perform more poorly on exams when they are several weeks removed from receiving food-stamp benefits. So, it's not just whether students are food insecure that influences test scores, but the likelihood that they have received support and how recently they received that support. Heissel, et. al. found that "children displayed a statistically significant increase in cortisol level in anticipation of high-stakes testing. Large decreases and large increases in cortisol were associated with underperformance on the high-stakes test." Acute stress leads to a large increase in cortisol, which has a direct negative effect on performance. And trauma, which often leads to dissociation, can cause a significant decrease in cortisol, also leading to lower performance. COVID-19 has certainly exacerbated trauma and anxiety around performance and testing. But the students struggling the most now are the ones most likely to have been struggling even before the pandemic. And those students (and so many of us) will likely continue to struggle.

Grades are more than just a bureaucratic abuse. I don't

use the word "abuse" lightly. I was a victim of abuse, and I'm bothered when I see the word "abuse" used as a metaphor. The voices of students, and the specific stories I've heard from students over the years, inhabit my work. Over the 23 years I've done research on grades and assessment, I've talked to hundreds of students about their educational experiences and hundreds of teachers about their experiences as students. I've heard from too many students who didn't get help when they were struggling:

> Part of the reason why I never asked for help was because I saw what my professors thought of those who did.

> I dropped out of college, in large part due to the hoops I had to jump through to get my disabilities recognized.

> It's a lot easier to stay motivated when you're not made to feel like you're stupid or a liar. It's a lot easier to focus on studying when you're not focused on having to justify yourself.

I often begin workshops about grades and assessment with the questions, "how does it feel to grade? how does it feel to be graded?" The answers I've gotten back have been startling. And, even where I find myself unsurprised by the answers, I am struck by the emotional language and by the accounts of trauma that arise within almost every conversation I've had about grades.

Grades are an invention with very specific

sociohistorical motivations and effects. Conversations about grades are, ultimately, conversations about power, which is why they are so often fraught, especially given how many of us have specific traumatic experiences of both grading and being graded.

A few years ago, I read a *New York Times* article that summarized the findings of a recent study. The title alone was enough to clench my stomach: "When Report Cards Go Out on Fridays, Child Abuse Increases on Saturdays, Study Finds." The study (specifically of primary-school-aged children) tracked calls made to the Florida Department of Children and Families child abuse hotline alongside dates when report cards were released by public schools throughout the state. The increase in abuse following the release of a report card was pronounced when the report cards were released on a Friday, as opposed to other days of the week. This finding led one of the researchers to offer a "practical solution" (in their account of the study to *The New York Times*): release report cards earlier in the week. Nowhere in the study itself or in *The New York Times* article does the grading system itself get a sufficient sidelong glance.

What kind of assessment approach does our current moment warrant? How do we address the fact that grades as a system disrupt the already fragile communities we are working to build in education? How do we push back against those systems without putting ourselves and our own livelihood at risk? In the face of rules and restrictions that seem insurmountable, what is our ethical responsibility to students?

· · · · ·

In *Education for Critical Consciousness*, Paulo Freire describes "dialogue" as "a horizontal relationship" that pushes back actively upon "vertical relationships," which he describes as "loveless, arrogant, hopeless, mistrustful, and acritical." This is the work of centering students, but not at the expense of teachers. Both must play an active role in and through this process. In *Pedagogy of the Oppressed*, he writes,

> A revolutionary leadership must accordingly practice co-intentional education. Teachers and students (leadership and people), co-intent on reality, are both Subjects, not only in the task of unveiling that reality, and thereby coming to know it critically, but in the task of re-creating that knowledge.

Co-intentional education is the shared examination of education with the goal of making space for teachers and students to define and redefine that space together. Our pedagogies become something we develop with (not for) students. This depends on each of us being what Freire calls "teacher-student with students-teachers," teaching each other, "mediated by the world, by the cognizable objects which in banking education are 'owned' by the teacher." Freire's use of the word "owned" here is important, because so many of the bureaucracies of education, grades in particular, function within a system of currency (where grades and GPAs have something akin to "exchange rates"). It isn't enough to empower students within that system (and perhaps fruitless even as an attempt); rather, students must be drawn into the construction and reconstruction of that system.

Freire is not speaking explicitly about assessment here. Students becoming "readers of their world" means they can critically interpret their material and political circumstances in order to make effective change. Assessment is a tool teachers can use in education to help (or hinder) this process. There is little room for agency or critical interpretation of material and political circumstances when power structures and crude hierarchies are reproduced or reinforced within education, with grades as the most direct mechanism for this. Simply, students can't learn to make effective change in their world from within an educational system they are discouraged from interrogating and powerless to change. Drawing students into critical conversation about assessment, then, is a way of helping them become *readers of their world*, but also, *readers of their own education*. This is a necessary precursor for co-intentional education.

The work of drawing students into the construction of courses, curricula, and assessment is especially important for students who are marginalized by institutions and systems, and for students who have trauma associated with their education. As a disabled, queer student, I might have attempted to assert agency over my own education, but almost always in the face of systems designed to strip me of that agency. Entering into conversation about my power as a student within those systems would have been predicated on my full personhood being recognized and acknowledged, which I have occasionally felt personally throughout my education, but never structurally. And, now, as a white male teacher with a different relationship to power in a classroom, I can grapple with my own educational history while also interrogating my own privilege and working to dismantle the structures I currently benefit from. I can only do this effectively if I do it alongside the students, and colleagues, with whom I work.

It's far too rare that teachers (or educational institutions) bring students fully into conversation about the what, how, and why of teaching. In my own practice, I have asked students to reflect on their own learning, and to grade themselves. The work of metacognition and self-reflection, though, means more than just having students process their learning; it means asking them (and ceding space for them to) engage in much deeper questions about education and the nature of educational institutions. We need to do intentional, critical work to dismantle traditional and standardized approaches to assessment. We can't do this work without understanding the specific contexts of the students we work with. For our work to be equitable, we can't merely ask students to grade themselves, but must work together to interrogate and dismantle grades as a system.

## 11

# Ungrading for Equity

"There is consensus in the literature about the benefits of a student's sense of belonging. Researchers suggest that higher levels of belonging lead to increases in GPA, academic achievement, and motivation." ~ Carey Borkoski

Over the last several years, many of us have found ourselves feeling isolated and alone. I know this is how many of the students I work with are feeling. This is how I am feeling. I have heard from teachers around the world that they aren't sure they want to be teachers anymore if this is what the work continues to look and feel like. I have heard from faculty members who feel overwhelmed by administrative indecision and continuing bureaucratic hurdles. I have talked to faculty who are seeing their institutions dismantled by a hostile state government. I have talked to students who have found the challenges of just living have made their schoolwork an afterthought. And I have also talked to students who feel increased anxiety about their schoolwork, grades, and GPAs, because these have become so conflated with their futures.

Many of the students we work with don't know where they will find their next meal. The most marginalized students at our institutions are finding themselves and their work increasingly policed — by faculty members, by administrative policies, by ed-tech "solutions," and by the actual police. The majority of faculty members in higher education are precariously employed. And many are afraid their institutions might close. Or, like me, they worked at institutions that have already closed.

As humans, as teachers, and as members of learning communities, we need to look around and be honest about the damage the last several years have wrought. More institutions will close. Staff will be laid off. Students will become sick. Cameras will be installed in classrooms, and disabled students will be made into flies on the wall for live-streamed lectures. Teachers will require homeless students to turn on their cameras during Zoom sessions. Some of those students will be marked absent if they refuse.

The moves back toward supposed "business as usual" have been made at the expense of marginalized students, staff, and faculty. We need to talk openly about different ways forward. And we need to be patient with ourselves and with each other.

At the heart of my pedagogical approach is a belief that pedagogy, and especially assessment, needs to be a conversation, a "critical dialogue," in the words of Paulo Freire. The classroom is a place for students and teachers to ask hard questions of one another, working together to reimagine the project of education, in order to help students (and teachers) become full agents in that education and in the broader culture in which they live.

Equity in education starts with small, human acts:

- Walk campus to assess accessibility of common spaces and classrooms. Accessible desks in each classroom don't do much good if students can't get to them because the rooms are overcrowded.

- Include a basic needs statement in your syllabus that directs students to resources and encourages them to talk to you if they need help. Don't bury the statement at the end. Lead with it.

- Make sure there's a simple and well-advertised process for students, faculty, and staff to change their names in institutional systems and that chosen names are what appear on course rosters and ID cards.

- Regularly invite campus community into hard conversations about equity and access. For example, frank discussion of gender and race bias in grading and course evaluations.

As much as this book is about grades, it has to be about so much more. When I run workshops about grades, we end up spending a good deal of time talking and writing about who are students are, what they need to be successful, and the kinds of relationships we want to build in education. Specifically, I ask,

> Who do you teach? What do you know about your students? Who are they? How are they changing? What do they want from their education? What barriers do they face?

Then, I have us think about what we most need to communicate to our students:

> What work do you value from students? What will you contribute (as the teacher)? What does success look like in your class? How (as the teacher) will you know when you've seen it? What is the students' collective role in constructing the course? How will you show care for your students? How will you show care for yourself?

As a teacher, starting from a place of care is human, but it's also pedagogical. Julianne Holt-Lunstad, et. al. write, "There is robust evidence that social isolation and loneliness significantly increase risk for premature mortality, and the magnitude of the risk exceeds that of many leading health indicators." In order to build and support community, we must be willing to acknowledge trauma members of that community have and will experience.

*Learning for Justice* offers "A Trauma-Informed Approach to Teaching Through Coronavirus," which is as relevant now as it was in 2020. They argue we need to:

- Establish a routine and maintain clear communication.
- Prioritize relationships and wellbeing over compliance.
- Actively encourage and support a sense of safety, connectedness, and hope.
- Acknowledge that trauma is not distributed equally.

Establishing clear communication shouldn't be focused primarily on clarifying policies or instructions. What's most important is that students know what to do if they're struggling and where they can go for help. In "The Single Most Essential Requirement in Designing a Fall Online Course," Cathy Davidson writes, "From everything we know about learning, if the trauma is not addressed, accounted for, and built into the course design, we fail. Our students fail."

I'm often asked if ungrading is an equitable practice. Can pushing back against grades do harm to BIPOC students, neurodiverse students, non-traditional adult students? The question gives me pause when I hear it, because so many folks are unwilling to turn the same critical eye at grades. Grades are widely accepted as effective (or, at least, meaningful), even if much of the research indicates otherwise. Certainly, making any dramatic changes to our pedagogies without considering our marginalized students can do harm, but ungrading is an equitable practice because *grades do harm*. And marginalized students are the students most harmed by grades. Finding ways to reduce that harm, and to begin to dismantle grades as a system, is imperative if equity or justice is our goal.

Some neurodiverse students rely on extrinsic motivation or structure, but neurodiverse students are not a monolith, and ungrading is not at odds with structure. It asks hard questions of structures in education that do harm, like grades, arbitrary deadlines, standardized testing, ranking students against one another, inflexible policies, etc. One big problem of traditional grades is that they structure much of education.

Removing grades, though, doesn't remove structure,

just one kind of problematic structure. Adding flexibility for students and teachers also doesn't remove structure. I'm disabled, neurodiverse, and need both flexibility and structure to succeed. Flexibility and structure are not at odds. Care and structure are not at odds. There are lots of mechanisms better than grades at providing structure for learners: a clear schedule, concise descriptions of class activities, clear ways to ask for help or feedback, community architecture that makes it easy for students to connect with each other. There are better structures than grades to support struggling students and teachers: student services, faculty development, a living wage for teachers, clear and direct communication between teachers and students, supports for collaboration and community rather than competition.

Structure, clear expectations, and boundaries are all good when we're working to build and support community, trust, etc. At the same time, flexibility helps support diverse and marginalized students (and can also make the work of assessment easier for diverse and marginalized faculty). Flexibility can mean removing rigid due dates to create space for students to do work as they're able, or acknowledging and valorizing different kinds of participation, or offering students multiple paths to choose from as they work through a course. The key is to resist the notion that the shape of teaching and learning should be fixed in advance and standardized.

We need to re-examine our pedagogies when we remove grades, because grades (control, compliance, over reliance on extrinsic motivation) have too often been at the foundation of those pedagogies. Removing individual acts of grading without doing that larger work can leave grades as a system still mostly intact.

None of this happens all at once. And there is no one right first step. We can't snap our fingers and dismantle grades as a system. I've been using alternative approaches to assessment for 23 years. I haven't put a grade on a single piece of student work during that time, but the grade still hovers over every classroom I've taught in, because the system of grades is insidious. We can start by having conversations and asking hard questions of each other, and of ourselves. Or by minimizing the harm of grades (making them less arbitrary, bringing students into the process, etc.).

Some tenets we can follow when designing for equity and care:

**We have to start by seeing students as full humans**, fully acknowledging their context and history. This requires structural change. Students can't be rows in a spreadsheet. A harm-reduction approach to assessment requires that we see each student (and each teacher) as unique, and that we see basic needs and pedagogical needs as inextricably linked. Static best practices, inflexible models, and stock curricula won't help us.

**We have to design for our most marginalized students:** disabled students, chronically ill students, Black students, Indigenous students, queer students, students facing housing and food-insecurity, etc. We need to write flexible policies, imagine new ways forward, for students already struggling, already facing exclusion.

**We need to anticipate rather than merely accommodating.** It is our legal obligation to offer accommodations for students with disabilities; however, our work should go further toward creating flexible spaces that anticipate the needs of diverse students. The students struggling the most are the ones least likely to ask for help, the ones least likely to know what accommodations are available or how to secure them.

**No learning is neatly quantifiable.** Not all learning will be visible to teachers or institutions. Student work can't be columns in a spreadsheet. Policing behavior, tracking attention, and algorithmic surveillance are not teaching.

**The work of teachers is precarious.** The context and subject positions of teachers impact how we will and can do our work. Teachers need adequate preparation, support, and compensation. To administrators wanting to "innovate", I say, *start by paying all teachers a living wage.*

Instead of rewarding competition, pitting teachers and staff against one another, and normalizing bullying, **institutions need to structurally support collaboration.** If there is no way to compensate and valorize co-teaching, that's a structural defect.

**Bringing students and teachers more fully into dialogue about assessment** (and about education more broadly) is the most important, and most radical, change we can work toward. And if students don't show up to these conversations, we need to ask ourselves what we've done to make them feel unwelcome.

These tenets can translate into practices: Start with hello, how are you?, Remind students a rug won't get pulled out from under them, create multiple points of entry, ask students to reflect on their own learning, etc. However, we ultimately need more conversations and fewer policies. Teaching should be about encouraging student learning not policing behavior. We can set boundaries, but we should keep our focus on natural consequences, not arbitrary ones, leaning into social contracts rather than lesson plans, rubrics, and grade books.

## 12

## Frequently Asked Questions

When talking with other educators, I frequently pose the question, "why do we grade?" The most common answer is, "because we have to." Nobody has ever told me, "because we want to," or "because grades are good." Most teachers seem to implicitly understand that something is wrong with our systems for grades and assessment. But there are lots of obstacles (many systemic, some personal) to changing how we do this work.

Over the years, I've gotten lots of questions about the what, why, and how of my own approach. These are some of those questions and my answers.

*Have you ever felt pressure from above to grade? If so, how did you overcome this pressure? What if I'm contingent, precarious, sessional, adjunct?*

Academic freedom (like the ability to make critical decisions about our teaching practices) must extend to precarious teachers.

Each institution where I've worked has had a different set of rules, structures, and norms for assessment. Navigating those hurdles (and institutional cultures) has been a challenge. I've been contingent for much of my teaching career, 11 of 23 years. During that time, I never put grades on student work, but it took me over a decade to start talking as openly as I am here about my approach. Some coping strategies that have worked for me: (1) I make sure my pedagogy is well-researched; (2) I bring students into the conversation about my approach; (3) I figure out what the firm rules are and follow them. We usually internalize way more restrictions than are actually there.

In fact, conventional approaches to grading are usually at direct odds with our institutional missions. So I look to those missions when advocating for teachers to have autonomy in their decisions about their approaches to assessment.

*Does ungrading make students anxious?*

Students sometimes start from a place of anxiety about

the removal of grades (because they've been conditioned to see them as markers of success, even if other things actually work better as markers of learning). It's important to acknowledge the real anxiety students feel about grades, about not grades, about performance, and about external perceptions of their performance. We can work to acknowledge, address, and alleviate that anxiety, but it won't just go away.

The key, I think, is making sure students believe us, that they aren't worried a rug will be pulled out from under them. This means teachers have to start by cultivating a sense of trust in the classroom. And building trust is hard. What I've found is that talking about the anxiety usually alleviates most of it. I used to talk with students about assessment on the first day of a course, but I've moved this conversation later into the term, usually when students are working on their first self-reflection. I try to follow the students' lead. If they need the conversation earlier, individually or as a group, we have it.

As long as I've been teaching, I still tweak my approach every single time. And the approach has to emerge from conversation with students about their specific contexts.

*Does ungrading affect the scores students give you on course evaluations?*

Generally, I think my pedagogical approach has helped my course evaluations (particularly my emphasis on compassionate and flexible pedagogies).

My scores on course evaluation questions specifically about grading have depended on how well the questions were phrased to allow for my approach. At one of my previous institutions, for example, the specific wording was: "The instructor provided clear criteria for grading" and "the instructor returned graded materials within a reasonable amount of time, considering the nature of the assignment." The words "criteria" and "returned graded materials" are out of sync with my approach. Much of the "criteria" in my courses is determined by students, and I neither "grade" materials, nor "return" them in any conventional way. So, it's unsurprising to me that I often score below department and college averages for these questions, even though my scores for all other questions is above department and college averages.

Course evaluations are a perfect example of how pedagogical decisions can be baked into administrative structures at an institution. This is, in my view, a direct threat to academic freedom. As we critically examine how we're grading students, we must also take a hard look at institutional assessment mechanisms for courses and instructors. Ultimately, the problem is the way course evaluations are designed, not ungrading as an approach. But it's important to acknowledge that course evaluations have a direct impact on the livelihood of teachers, particularly those who are already marginalized or working precariously. And, as problematic as they are, course evaluations are one of the few institutional mechanisms students have for offering feedback on their education. So, we can't teach (or talk about teaching) as though course evaluations don't exist.

*Do you know if ungrading is sometimes used for STEM courses?*

Ungrading and alternative assessment work well across disciplines, age groups, and at all levels of education. Certainly, lots of modifications are necessary depending on the specific context. Different disciplines call for different approaches.

I know quite a few STEM folks who ungrade in various ways. Some specific stuff I've seen work in STEM classes: project-based learning with self-assessment, process notebooks (like lab reports but with an emphasis on metacognition), and collaborative exams. Exams, in particular, are at their best when they are formative tools for learning, not just standardized mechanisms for summative (or end-of-learning) assessment. Collaborative exams allow students opportunities to learn from and teach each other. Open-book and self-graded exams are not as good at sorting or ranking students, but they are often better tools for learning.

Some disciplines require students to take a licensure exam or something similar at the end of the program. I'd say the best preparation is not to repeat an identical experience over and over in anticipation, but to help students get under the hood of the exam they're preparing for. Taking the exam in a low-stakes and low-pressure environment gives students the space they need to think and talk openly about how the exam is structured, what it is attempting to measure, and where it fails to adequately capture what they're learning. Just because the students will be assessed later in a standardized, quantitative way doesn't mean we have to replicate that in our courses.

*How do you find the time to offer narrative feedback to every single student?*

I used to offer tons of feedback in lieu of grades. I realized, though, that this feedback was often presumptuous and still centered my voice as the teacher. I now have students direct my feedback, asking them to tell me specifically when (and on what) they want feedback.

The students' own questions and perspectives guide my responses. And I leave the students alone when that's what they need for their process. I think the key is communicating *with* students and not *to* them. Even the idea of "feedback" is suspect to me, unless it goes both ways. In place of "feedback," I rely on Freire's idea of "dialogue."

My approach can take more time, especially when I'm planning a new course. But once the term begins, I'd say it takes less time. During the first 11 years that I was questioning traditional grading and assessment, I worked as an adjunct, teaching up to 9 classes each term at 4 institutions, with as many as 1000 students each year. Many of my approaches were developed specifically to address the sense of overwhelm that came with that course load. I wanted to spend less time grading and more time building relationships. I worked to foster a culture of self-reflection and feedback in my courses, so that students were able to support themselves and each other with me as a guide.

The bulk of my "grading" time, over the years, has been spent reading self-reflections, having conversations with students, and adapting our course on the fly as I get to know the students and what they need to be successful.

*I teach a class of 50, 100, 400 in a large lecture hall.*

*How can ungrading work in a course like that?*

I've taught traditional college classes with over 150 students, and I've taught non-traditional classes with many many more. What I've found is that trust and compassion scale. And allowing space for student agency scales.

Teaching metacognition and having students self-evaluate is just as effective (and more necessary) in large classes, where I can't possibly see inside the brain/process of each student. Reading students' self-reflection letters is what helps me "see" student learning in a large class, so that I know when they need support or feedback.

A few things that work well with large groups:

- Have students read about metacognition and invite open discussion about grading
- Incorporate several self-evaluations throughout the term asking students to reflect on and analyze their own work
- Write one letter to the class offering general feedback, noting trends, and responding to common questions
- Invite students to make individual appointments and reach out personally to those who are struggling
- Share (with permission) anonymized highlights

from self-reflections, including data re: grade distribution, and encourage conversation

- Adjust grades if necessary (especially to account for internalized bias), but otherwise submit the final grades students give themselves

With a group of 50, 100, or 400, I can't give the same amount of feedback that I would with a smaller group, so I do more talking and writing to the class as a whole. For me, not grading saves time. It doesn't mean I do less work. I just put my energy into other work that better supports student learning.

*Would you describe ungrading as a decolonizing, radical, progressive, feminist, critical pedagogical practice?*

Ungrading is a key part of my critical pedagogical approach, but it only works as a radical, decolonizing, feminist practice, if it's done carefully and alongside other critical pedagogical practices.

Grades reinforce teacher/student hierarchies (and institution/teacher hierarchies) while exacerbating other problematic power relationships. Women, POC, disabled people, neurodiverse people are all ill-served by a destructive culture of grading and assessment.

Ungrading can unsettle power dynamics in productive ways, but it can also reinforce structural biases if those biases aren't explicitly acknowledged and accounted for. Toward this end, I share and discuss data about bias in grading with students. I also have a responsibility to spend time actively challenging my biases and reflecting on my own privilege/marginalization.

I believe an actively anti-racist, anti-misogynist, anti-ableist approach is more effective than supposedly "objective" approaches like blind grading (which just maintain the status quo, rather than accounting for privilege or marginalization).

The biggest problems arise, in my view, when we devise learning outcomes, determine policies, and craft assessments before we've even met the specific students we're working with. Too many of our approaches treat students like they're interchangeable and fail to recognize their complexity. Not every student begins at the same place, nor is it even reasonable to imagine every student can, or should, end up at the same place. Ultimately, critical pedagogical practice has to acknowledge the background, context, and embodied experience that both teachers and students bring to the classroom. Any predetermined standardized metric will almost necessarily fail at that.

*How do you motivate students? If you aren't grading, but your colleagues are, won't students de-prioritize the work for your classes?*

Students do sometimes prioritize other graded courses over mine (although it is much rarer than people are often worried it would be). And I'm okay with that. Honestly, it seems like good time management for students to prioritize work with a rigid deadline and high stakes. Our education system has trained students very well to work within structures that emphasize grades, points, quantification, and extrinsic motivators.

I'm trying to encourage intrinsic motivation, and it's difficult for that to compete with extrinsic motivators (for me too). But when students clear the decks of other work and turn to work for my classes, they can do so with gusto. And it is common for students in my classes to work harder for those classes than any others (but in their own time), because they have a reason better than points. (To be clear, a focus on intrinsic motivators doesn't mean eliminating all extrinsic motivators.)

I also find that it's easier to have honest conversations with students, where we challenge each other in meaningful ways, if I'm not regularly grading them.

*If I'm thinking about ungrading, how should I start?*

As I've mentioned, ungrading works best when we also rethink due dates, policies, syllabi, and assignments — when we ask students to do work that has intrinsic value and authentic audiences. However, it starts with teachers just talking to students about grades. None of the other techniques described here are necessary beyond that one. Demystifying grades (and the culture around them) helps give students a sense of ownership over their own education. Martin Bickman writes, "We often ignore the best resource for informed change, one that is right in front of our noses every day — our students, for whom the most is at stake." Even if you change nothing else about how you approach assessment, start simply by having a single conversation with students about grades and let your approach evolve from there.

## 13

# What if We Didn't Grade?: A Bibliography

In the last several chapters, I proposed some possible first steps toward ungrading, specifically that the best way to begin is through open conversation with students about grades. Perhaps, just as important, is that teachers start by having these conversations more often with each other. There has always been a reflective layer to my teaching, a community of colleagues and co-teachers I turn to for intense discussions about the nature of teaching, both in philosophy and practice. In higher education, this kind of pedagogical community is unfortunately rare. With so many teachers working contingently and most receiving little formal preparation for the work of the teaching, where and when can we safely ask the question, "What if we didn't grade?"

When I talk to other faculty (and students) about grades, I start with questions about the what, why, and how of grading. Our answers influence all the other work we do:

- Why do we grade? How does it feel to be graded? What do we want grading to do (or not do) in our classes (for students or teachers)?

- What do letter grades mean? Do they have intrinsic meaning, or is their value purely extrinsic? Does assessment mean something different when it is formative rather than summative?

- How does feedback function in relation to grades? Does grading create a power structure that frustrates authentic relationships? To what extent should teachers be readers of student work (as opposed to evaluators)?

- What would happen if we didn't grade? What would be the benefits? What issues would this raise for students and/or teachers? What kind of structural obstacles would we face?

- What would it look like to design adaptively, to listen more intently, to reimagine teaching as a creative act we take up together with students?

These questions are what hum beneath the writing that is foundational to my thinking about grades. Some of the works I find myself returning to again and again do get to the nuts and bolts of radical assessment, but the focus is more squarely on rethinking the structures in education that short-circuit the work of teaching and learning.

**Foundations**

> Alfie Kohn, "The Case Against Grades"
> Alfie Kohn, *Punished by Rewards: The Trouble with Gold Stars, Incentive Plans, A's, Praise, and Other Bribes*

I struggled to pick just two books or articles to recommend from Alfie Kohn. I've recently finished another excellent book by him, *Unconditional Parenting: Moving From Rewards and Punishment to Love and Reason*, which is also well worth reading. Kohn's "The Case Against Grades" is one of the pieces I return to most often, and it captures much of what I appreciate about his work. His writing is clear and straightforward, while also turning our most common presumptions about education on their head. Kohn's central tenets are: "Grades tend to diminish students' interest in whatever they're learning"; "Grades create a preference for the easiest possible task"; and "Grades tend to reduce the quality of students' thinking." His survey of almost 100 years of research is compelling, but his statements of what should be obvious (but isn't) are what make his work so necessary and vital: "We have to be willing to challenge the conventional wisdom, which in this case means asking not how to improve grades but how to jettison them once and for all."

> Peter Elbow, "Grading Student Writing: Making It Simpler, Fairer, Clearer"
> Peter Elbow, "Ranking, Evaluating, Liking: Sorting Out Three Forms of Judgment"

Peter Elbow is one of the very first pedagogical theorists that I read, and much of what I learned from him remains central to my approach. Much of his work is about the teaching of writing but is nonetheless extremely relevant to every discipline. Two things I find particularly valuable from Elbow: (1) the concept of minimal grading, about which he writes, "I would rather put my effort into trying to figure out which activities will lead to learning than into trying to measure the exact quality of the final product students turn in"; and (2) the notion that "liking" our students' work could be both pleasurable and also an effective pedagogical strategy. Elbow writes, "Good teachers see what is only potentially good, they get a kick out of mere possibility — and they encourage it."

> Asao Inoue, "A Social Justice Framework for Anti-Racist

Writing Assessment: Labor-Based Grading Contracts"
Cathy Davidson, "Contract Grading and Peer Review"

Asao Inoue's and Cathy Davidson's experiments with contract grading are different in many ways but both of them have helped drive much of my thinking about this approach. My concern about contract grading at its surface is that it runs the risk of centering grades more than decentering them. However, Inoue and Davidson show how the approach can be used to raise critical conversations about what grades are, how they make meaning, and how they can be interrogated in the service of marginalized students.

Asao Inoue writes that labor-based grading contracts specifically "avoid many of the harmful and racist consequences of conventional grading ecologies by not using the dominant white discourse as the standard for grades." The piece from him above is a brief handout that introduces the work he describes at length in his book, *Antiracist Writing Assessment Ecologies: Teaching and Assessing Writing for a Socially Just Future*.

Soraya Chemaly, "All Teachers Should Be Trained To Overcome Their Hidden Biases"

This relatively short piece is filled with links to research into the problem(s) of bias in education, and also standardized grades. For example, she shares studies that show "teachers spend up to two thirds of their time talking to male students; they also are more likely to interrupt girls but allow boys to talk over them. ... When teachers ask questions, they direct their gaze towards boys more often, especially when the questions are open-ended." For anyone thinking about ungrading or inclusive pedagogies, I'd recommend opening and reading every single one of Chemaly's links. But I will also warn that some of the studies are more gut-wrenching than others. Grades are not a coincidence. Our systems for assessment reduce students to rows in a spreadsheet, to data points, and strip them of their humanity.

> Jeffrey Schinske and Kimberly Tanner, "Teaching More by Grading Less (or Differently)"

I often turn to this piece for its account of the history of grades in higher education. Every one of their sentences is packed with detail. They couple incisive commentary with refreshing (well-documented) statements like this one, "It would not be surprising to most faculty members that, rather than stimulating an interest in learning, grades primarily enhance students' motivation to avoid receiving bad grades." In spite of a rather bleak account of what grades have been and are becoming, the piece ends on an optimistic note, "One wonders how much more student learning might occur if instructors' time spent grading was used in different ways."

**Other Points of Entry**

Asking students to be directly involved in the grading process and in helping dismantle grades as a system is an extension of my core teaching philosophy, which is grounded in the work of critical pedagogy. My approach to ungrading has arisen as much from that core philosophy as it has from stuff I've read about grades and assessment. So, I'll end by pointing to two incredible books, one of the first pedagogy books I read, and one of the books I read most recently. Neither of these books is about grades specifically (nor really has grading as a focus at all), but they are exactly about core philosophies, and thus a wonderful place to begin.

> bell hooks, *Teaching to Transgress*
> "The classroom remains the most radical space of possibility in the academy."

> Kevin Gannon, *Radical Hope: a Teaching Manifesto*
> "Pedagogy cannot be neutral. ... Neutrality is a luxury of the comfortable; in these uncomfortable times, our students and our academic communities need more from us."

Ungrading is not as simple as just removing grades. The

word "ungrading" suggests that we need to do intentional, critical work to dismantle traditional and standardized approaches to assessment. There's a lot to read, certainly, but no neat and tidy point of entry. Rather, each teacher (and each student) must find their own ways into the work. The works cited at the end of this book offers more potential beginnings.

## 14

# Do We Need the Word "Ungrading"?

While I'd used the word in workshops and talks as early as 2003, I first explicitly published about "ungrading" in an October 2017 piece titled "Why I Don't Grade" (included in this collection), where I wrote, "Grades are currency for a capitalist system that reduces teaching and learning to a mere transaction. Grading is a massive co-ordinated effort to take humans out of the educational process." In that piece, I "withheld the mechanics of ungrading deliberately, because I agree with Alfie Kohn who writes, 'When the how's of assessment preoccupy us, they tend to chase the why's back into the shadows.'" My own definition of the term has evolved, but I've consistently argued that it's problematic to reduce ungrading to a zeitgeist, a trendy set of decontextualized best practices.

## Undoing the Grade

There is no neat and tidy thing we can all do tomorrow to obliterate grades. That simply isn't the system, culture, or labor conditions that many of us work within. Again, different approaches work for different teachers in different disciplines in different ways at different times. Some have suggested the word "ungrading" is a misnomer, because most students are still getting final grades, but I'd say it's the exact right word to describe the two key components of my definition: (1) an active and ongoing critique of grades as a system and (2) the decision to do what we can, depending on our labor conditions, to carefully dismantle that system.

I believe part of the role of a teacher is to stand in the gap between institutions and students in order to call out and mitigate harm. There are specific things we can do in our approach to assessment that can have profound effects on our work and on the relationships we develop with students and the relationships students develop with each other. But, ultimately, ungrading is a systemic critique. The problem of conflating ungrading with "not grading" is that it ignores the precarity of teachers and the labor issues in education, reframing grades as a moral issue, instead of a structural one.

Grading is a mechanism for subjugating students, and also a tool that institutions use to control teachers. However we might try to reinvent them, grades are saturated, sticky with their faults: grades reflect bias, they do disproportionate harm to marginalized students and teachers, they don't communicate coherently, they don't adequately measure what we value most about learning, they contribute to a culture of competition in education, and an over-reliance on extrinsic motivation short-circuits intrinsic motivation. To reiterate, the problem is not individual teachers who grade, but the systems and structures that fundamentally distort the goals of assessment and make grades compulsory. The problem is an insidious culture of quantitative and standardized assessment that pits students and teachers against one another — and that compels teachers (especially those of us in contingent positions) to work in ways at odds with our individual teaching philosophies and (often) the mission statements of the institutions where we work.

I don't think it's a coincidence that ungrading is so often reduced to a static set of best practices or confused with "not grading" — or, worse, confused with teachers "not doing our jobs." These are ways to instrumentalize teaching, demean teachers, and devalue the work of teaching. Less than half of higher education teachers get meaningful or significant preparation for the work of teaching as graduate students or as new faculty ("The Human Work of Higher Education Pedagogy"). This is a fatal structural flaw. Collaboration between teachers is actively discouraged. Most institutions have no policies in place to support collaborative teaching. This is a fatal structural flaw. 70% of faculty in higher education are contingent or adjunct. This is a fatal structural flaw. The work of teachers at all levels of education is increasingly precarious and our ability to carve our own paths through the work is under attack. How do we support struggling students if the bulk of teachers have little structural power to do or advocate for that work? How do we teach from a place of care if our school (and its community) is threatened by a corrupt state government? Or if we are marginalized and not getting necessary support from our institutions? How do we reimagine assessment when grades are so thoroughly baked into our educational systems? How do we reimagine assessment when quantitative and standardized assessment is also weaponized against teachers?

We need to start by trusting teachers. Institutions and administrators should not be making critical pedagogical decisions for teachers. Institutions should not universally adopt technologies (like learning management systems) or adhere strictly to models (like Quality Matters) that make critical pedagogical decisions for teachers. We need to start by trusting students. Every dollar we invest in proctoring software, plagiarism detection tools, and other policing technologies needs to be reinvested in student support and faculty development. Ungrading means acknowledging context and the material circumstances of students and teachers, then doing whatever we can to push back against broken systems that feel (but sometimes aren't) immovable.

In most formal education, grades are *a* (if not *the*) structuring principle of institutions, institutional cultures, and educational technologies. There is no easy switch we can flip to turn off grades. The work of ungrading is to ask questions, have hard conversations, point to the fundamental inequities of grades, push for systemic change, and to mitigate or obstruct harm that grading, and grades as a system, do to marginalized students and precarious educators. There are lots of entry points to that work.

I've never been attached to the word "ungrading." It has had rhetorical purpose, sparking conversations about the exact things that some find troubling about the word. And it continues to have rhetorical purpose, as those conversations have gotten louder and more imperative. For me, the work of ungrading is to question tacit assumptions/buzzwords and critique harmful labor/learning conditions. The word catalyzes a set of conversations that are increasingly necessary. However, I don't see "ungrading" as a catch all to include every kind of alternative assessment. One word/idea shouldn't be a monolith gobbling up everything around it, especially a word like "ungrading," which is currently being used productively by lots of different people in lots of different ways. Gatekeeping is the single most harmful feature of academia. When ideas congeal into a "movement," "club," or an exclusive "community," lines too often get drawn, people bully each other for status, and already marginalized people end up further marginalized.

62% of higher education faculty/staff stated they'd been bullied or witnessed bullying vs. 37% in the general population. People from minority communities are disproportionately bullied. (Hollis 2012)

51% of college students claimed to have seen another student being bullied by a teacher at least once and 18% claimed to have been bullied themselves by a teacher. (Marraccini 2013)

At this point, what's important to me is the work — teachers and students collaborating to support, defend, and (where necessary) transform education. This isn't "big tent" work. At this point, it's "humongous tent" work.

Here are just a few of the approaches and philosophies I've mentioned in this book that came before and/or sit alongside the current conversation about ungrading: minimal grading, labor-based grading contracts, specifications grading, self-reflection, authentic assessment, and more. I think there's strategic value in having these conversations in the same room, but they aren't the same conversation.

These conversations also aren't new. As I've previously written, grades have a history, even if it's a relatively recent one (just over 200 years, and only popularized in the last 50). Ungrading also has a history, and it's important to not lose touch with that. It's a field, not just a moment, not a zeitgeist, not just a stack of practices. As long as there have been grades, there have been productive critiques of grades (and the structures that reinforce them):

Virginia Woolf writes, "To sacrifice a hair of the head of your vision, a shade of its colour, in deference to some Headmaster with a silver pot in his hand or to some professor with a measuring-rod up his sleeve, is the most abject treachery."

bell hooks writes about "continual self-evaluation" both of a student by the student and of a teacher by the teacher.

Ruha Benjamin asks, "what are the responsibilities of educators and educational institutions in a context where this is a deliberate campaign to break society, erode mutuality, grind down our ability to care for one another, eat away at any notion of a collective good, and destroy the institutions upon which our society depends?"

Asao B. Inoue argues that Labor-based grading contracts "avoid many of the harmful and racist consequences of conventional grading ecologies by not using the dominant white discourse as the standard for grades."

John and Evelyn Dewey write in *Schools of To-Morrow*, "Unless the mass of workers are to be blind cogs and pinions in the apparatus they employ, they must have some understanding of the physical and social facts behind and ahead of the material and appliances with which they are dealing."

We have to look back even as we look forward.

We need to carefully unpack, ideally together with students, the history, philosophy, technologies, and practices of grading. Then, we can knock down the barriers that keep teachers and students from working together to actively reimagine how we do assessment in education.

## Good-For-Some-People-In-Some-Contexts Practices

Best practices need to give way to good-for-some-people-in-some-contexts practices. In that spirit, I will end here with a few ways we might begin this work:

**Change how we talk about assessment.** Ungrading works best as part of a holistic pedagogical practice. In *Hacking Assessment*, Starr Sackstein writes, "The language associated with grading often has a negative connotation that shuts the learning down." Use words like "ask" or "invite," rather than "submit" or "required." Encourage students to talk about their expectations for their work, rather than centering our own.

**Invite students to a conversation about grades.** Ask students how being graded makes them feel, how it affects their motivation. As a group, read and discuss a piece like Alfie Kohn's "The Case Against Grades."

**Grade less stuff, grade less often, grade more simply.** Create space in our courses for discovery and experimentation. Use grading scales that feel less arbitrary and communicate more clearly to students. Ask students to do work that we don't "collect."

**Encourage students to reflect on their own learning.** Even if we change nothing else about how we grade, we need to ask students when and how they learn. Ask what barriers they face. Listen. And believe the answers.

**Necessary Practices**

Alongside these good-for-some-people-in-some-contexts practices, I've begun arguing for what I call "necessary practices." These are the things we must do now to make education more equitable, the hurdles we have to knock down as a precursor to the work of dismantling grades as a system. I encourage every administrator, teacher, and student to look carefully at their institution and ask what structural barriers get in the way of teaching and learning. Pedagogical work requires that we start by making our schools hospitable places, safe places.

**Pay teachers a living wage.** This includes academic staff, support staff, librarians, adjuncts, and substitute teachers.

**Know whether or not your students had breakfast.** Don't expect representative performance on high stakes assessments from students whose basic needs aren't met.

**Know whether your students have a safe place to live.** Don't assign homework, especially with a strict deadline, without acknowledging what it might mean for housing-insecure or homeless students.

**Work to minimize harm.** Compassion and trust are the things that should drive our pedagogies and our policies. Whatever the barriers and however we begin, it's our responsibility as educators to help identify and dismantle systems that do harm to students.

Finally, **we need to stop having conversations about the future of education without students in the room.** Ultimately, students should be drivers of the conversations we have in education about assessment, grades, and ungrading.

# Afterword: The End of Grades

SEAN MICHAEL MORRIS

I have this memory from my childhood, from elementary school. I must have been in kindergarten — or first grade at the latest — and my brother (five years older than me) was performing in the choir. My family had returned to the school in the evening to watch the performance and I recall it felt strange in the dark: empty hallways and classrooms, teachers standing about like normal adults (instead of teachers), the building somehow more public and less particular. The cafeteria had been transformed into a music hall, and all my brothers' classmates stood upon risers where earlier there had been lunch tables, spilled milk, peanut butter sandwiches, and kids trading snacks. The pungent smell of children with tin lunch boxes and sticky hands remained in the air.

I only remember one thing from the concert itself. I'm sure there were popular songs sung — some American childhood standards alongside a weird selection of contemporary music, and probably some medleys — but I don't remember the singing. What I remember is my brother and his best friend taking a bow. That they were the only kids who took a bow. It was choir horseplay, and kidding around; they had wide smiles on their faces and laughed at each other when they did it, while all the rest of the choir stood stock still listening to their parents' applause.

Add to that memory one more: my brother and his friend chastised by the music teacher for their horseplay. Taking a bow was not acceptable, not good manners, not what members of a choir were supposed to do. I don't know if my brother has these same memories, but I suspect they impacted his sense of play, pride, and what's appropriate nonetheless.

In a talk I gave some time ago, I remarked:

> Grades hamstring us by their very nature. Grades get soaked into the learning identity of the student who gets them ... [and] we continue to talk about grades long after they've ceased to matter because they mark us indelibly. ("When We Talk about Grades, We Are Talking about People")

The grades we get tell us something about who we are. No matter how much teachers talk about grades as representative of someone's work, or about rubrics as objective tools for measuring comprehension, the person who gets 100% feels differently about their capacity to learn and succeed than the person who gets 70%. The same goes for chastisements from music teachers, careless remarks from English professors, implicit gender bias in STEM classes.

I witnessed the impact of this — both with and without regard to grades — as a first year graduate writing teacher. That first semester, and every semester that followed, I heard stories from students about their elementary and secondary teachers who told them outright, "You'll never be a good writer," or "Writing isn't your thing," or "Let's just try to get through one essay, shall we?" And, of course, the punctuation at the end of those stories always came down to grades. Bad grades. Failing grades. But it started with the commentary, with the casual judgements of (probably overworked) teachers. The students telling these stories considered themselves bad at writing, failures. To come to my writing class was to confront a horror, a certainty of being inadequate, a time in their lives when trying to be better wouldn't amount to any success.

I think teachers generally don't know how intimidating they are, nor how permanent their judgements of a student can be. Summative comments about a person's work are formative lessons about that person's worth.

Ungrading doesn't change this, and that's because there's "larger work" that needs doing, as Jesse Stommel writes earlier in this book. "We need to re-examine our pedagogies when we remove grades, because grades (control, compliance, over reliance on extrinsic motivation) have too often been structuring those pedagogies" (p. 113).

But I would take this one step further — or perhaps one step closer. Because grading doesn't start with the teacher, it starts with a culture of expectations of excellence that oppresses everyone in education, from student to teacher and on up.

Grades are means to only one end: they are designed to keep people out. We mask them as progress reports, as neutral evaluation tools; but the point of grades is to tell someone whether they belong or not, whether they have earned belonging. An "A" or a 100% means a student is the closest to belonging as they can get: they are looked at by their teachers as someone they respect, someone intelligent or capable; and they are welcome in the classroom. But slip once, slip twice, and their standing is in peril, and in some cases only an act of forgiveness will maintain their status. A "good" student who begins earning low grades, doing unacceptable work or who, once or twice, fails the academic integrity test will need to start proving themselves all over again.

When we grade, we teach students to rely less on their own thoughts about their worth than upon ours; but in turn, we also learn to devalue self-reflection and self-knowledge, and instead accept the unspoken and ubiquitous dictum that our value is better assessed by another.

We do not grade but that we also grade ourselves. We do not assess except that we assess ourselves. An academe that perpetuates grades is is fueled by a culture of continual litmus testing, yardsticking — a culture of competition and self-competition, doubt and self-doubt, criticism in the name of bettering others and self-criticism in the name of bettering oneself. This is the trap of the double-blind peer review, this is the dissertation committee, this is the 7-year audition for tenure.

There is no upside here. There is no world in which establishing criteria for another person's worth does not also result in our establishing criteria for their worthlessness. And when we establish that criteria, we, also, become subject to it. We should not strive to be the purveyors of ignominy.

Just as grades are designed to keep people out, so is a culture of constant evaluation and judgment designed with the same intention. The idea that permission must be given to enter into a scholarly community, that arbitrary achievements like time spent in a classroom or the number of publications can certify a person as eligible for that community — we cannot think that ends when a person is granted access. Indeed, it doesn't; the battle for worth and respect is an ongoing one. Grading becomes integrated to one's experience of self.

Once we start grading, we never stop.

When my brother was chastised by his music teacher, he was subject to an expectation of excellence utterly unfair to a fifth grader. When students were afraid to enter my classroom and begin writing, they were likewise subject to the same unfairness. We need to dismantle the power of grades, and this means recognizing the ways in which we have, ourselves, suffered under that power.

Academics should not be terrified of one another's judgments, just as students should not be afraid of their teachers.

I have never been fond of the term "ungrading." Lexically, it does little to dismantle power or the centrality of grades. "Going gradeless" isn't much better. We need a new word, a new concept, to describe an approach that honors rather than evaluates. As Maxine Greene would encourage, we need to imagine things as they might be otherwise; in this case, a world where evaluation of others isn't part of the daily work of teachers, academics, or students. A world instead where worth is assumed —

where great worth is assumed — and where everyone is allowed to take a bow.

# Works Cited

Benjamin, Ruha. "Foreword." *Critical Digital Pedagogy: A Collection*. Hybrid Pedagogy, 2020.

Berthoff, Ann E. "Dialectical Notebooks and the Audit of Meaning." *The Journal Book*. Ed. Toby Fulwiler. Portsmouth, NH: Boynton/Cook, 1987.

Bickman, Martin. "Returning to Community and Praxis: A Circuitous Journey through Pedagogy and Literary Studies." *Pedagogy*. Vol. 10, no. 1, 2010, pp. 11-23.

Borkoski, Carey. "Cultivating Belonging." *AC&E Equity & Access journal*. November – December Issue. 2019.

Bowers, William J. *Student Dishonesty and its Control in College*. Columbia, 1966.

Burtis, Martha. "Neither Locked Out Nor Locked In." *The Fish Wrapper*. 5 June 2017.

Chemaly, Soraya. "All Teachers Should Be Trained to Overcome Their Hidden Biases." *Time*. 12 February 2015.

Collier, Amy. "Digital Sanctuary: Protection and Refuge on the Web?" *Educause*. 28 August 2017.

Cook, Lloyd Allen. *Community Backgrounds of Education: A Textbook in Educational Sociology*. Taylor & Francis, 2006.

Cotti, Chad, John Gordanier, and Orgul Ozturk. "When does it count? The timing of food stamp receipt and educational performance." *Economics of Education Review*. Vol. 66, 2018, pp. 40-50.

Danielewski, Mark Z. *House of Leaves*. Pantheon, 2000.

Davidson, Cathy. *Contract Grading and Peer Review*. HASTAC. 16 August 2015.

Davidson, Cathy. "How Do We Measure What Really Counts in the Classroom?" *Fast Company*. 20 September 2012.

Davidson, Cathy. *Now You See It*. Penguin Books, 2012.

Davidson, Cathy. "The Single Most Essential Requirement in Designing a Fall Online Course." *Humanities Commons*. 20 July 2020.

Dewey, John and Evelyn Dewey. *Schools of To-morrow*. Dent, 1915.

Dickinson, Emily. "From all the Jails the Boys and Girls." *The complete poems of Emily Dickenson*. Edited by Martha Dickenson Bianchi. Little, Brown, 1924.

Elbow, Peter. "Grading Student Writing: Making It Simpler, Fairer, Clearer." *New Directions for Teaching and Learning*. Vol. 69, 1997, pp. 127-40.

Elbow, Peter. "Ranking, Evaluating, and Liking: Sorting Out

Three Forms of Judgment." *College English.* Vol. 55, no. 2, 1993, pp. 187-206.

Fast, Amy [@fastcrayon]. "The saddest and most ironic practice in schools is how hard we try to measure how students are doing and how rarely we ever ask them." 28 March 2016.

Freire, Paulo. *Education for Critical Consciousness.* Bloomsbury, 2021.

Freire, Paulo. *Pedagogy of the Oppressed.* Translated by Myra Bergman Ramos. Penguin, 1970.

Gannon, Kevin. *Radical Hope.* West Virginia University Press, 2020.

Gilliard, Chris. "Pedagogy and the Logic of Platforms." *Educause.* 3 July 2017.

Goldrick-Rab, Sara and Jesse Stommel. "Teaching the Students We Have Not the Students We Wish We Had." *The Chronicle of Higher Education.* 10 December 2018.

Green, Maxine. "Teaching as Possibility: A Light in Dark Times." *Journal of Pedagogy, Pluralism, and Practice.* Vol. 1, no. 1, 1997.

Greene, Maxine. *Releasing the Imagination: Essays on Education, the Arts, and Social Change.* Jossey-Bass, 1995.

Heilweil, Rebecca. "Paranoia about cheating is making online education terrible for everyone." *Vox.* 4 May 2020.

Heissel, Jennifer A., Emma K. Adam, Jennifer L. Doleac, David N. Figlio, and Jonathan Meer. "Testing, Stress, and Performance: How Students Respond Physiologically to

High-Stakes Testing." *Education Finance and Policy*. Vol. 16, no. 2, 2021, pp. 183-208.

Hollis, Leah. *Bully in the Ivory Tower*. New York: Hollis, 2012.

Holt, John. *Instead of Education: Ways to Help People Do Things Better*. Sentient, 2004.

Holt-Lunstad, Julianne, Timothy B Smith, Mark Baker, Tyler Harris, and David Stephenson. "Loneliness and social isolation as risk factors for mortality: a meta-analytic review." *Perspectives on Psychological Science*. Vol. 10, no. 2, 2015.

hooks, bell. "Choosing the Margin as a Space of Radical Openness." *Framework: The Journal of Cinema and Media*. No. 36, 1989, pp. 15-23.

hooks, bell. *Teaching Critical Thinking*. Routledge, 2013.

hooks, bell. *Teaching to Transgress*. Routledge, 1994.

Inoue, Asao B. *Labor-Based Grading Contracts: Building Equity and Inclusion in the Compassionate Writing Classroom*. WAC Clearinghouse, 2023.

Inoue, Asao B. "A Grade-Less Writing Course That Focuses on Labor and Assessing." *First Year Composition: From Theory to Practice*. Eds. D. Teague and R. Lunsford. West Lafayette: Parlor Press, 2014.

Jacobs, Julia. "When Report Cards Go Out on Fridays, Child Abuse Increases on Saturdays, Study Finds." *New York Times*. 17 December 2018.

Kohn, Alfie. "The Case Against Grades." *Educational Leadership*. Vol. 69, no. 3., 2011, pp. 28-33.

Kohn, Alfie. *Punished by Rewards*. Boston: Houghton Mifflin, 1993.

Kohn, Alfie. "The Trouble With Rubrics." *English Journal*. Vol. 95, no. 4, 2006.

Lang, James M. *Cheating Lessons: Learning from Academic Dishonesty*. Harvard University Press, 2013.

Learning for Justice. "A Trauma-Informed Approach to Teaching Through Coronavirus." 23 March 2020.

Malouff, John M. and Einar B Thorsteinsson. "Bias in grading: A meta-analysis of experimental research findings." *Australian Journal of Education*. Vol. 60, no. 3, 2016.

Marraccini, Marisa E. *College Students' Perceptions of Professor Bullying*. University of Rhode Island, 2013.

McCabe, Donald L., Kenneth D. Butterfield, and Linda K. Treviño. *Cheating in College: Why Students Do It and What Educators Can Do about It*. The Johns Hopkins University Press, 2012.

Melville, Herman. "Bartleby, the Scrivener: A Story of Wall Street." *The Piazza Tales*. Dix & Edwards, 1856.

Morris, Sean Michael and Jesse Stommel. "If Freire Made a MOOC: Open Education as Resistance." *Hybrid Pedagogy*. 20 November 2014.

Morris, Sean Michael. "When We Talk about Grades, We Are

Talking about People." seanmichaelmorris.com. 9 June 2021.

Newton, Derek. "Another problem with shifting education online: cheating." *Washington Post.* 7 August 2020.

Nelson, Libby. "Black Students Were Hurt Most When Wellesley Tried to Control Grade Inflation." *Vox.* 13 March 2015.

Phelan, Julia. "Academic Integrity in the Age of Online Learning." Wiley, 2020.

Rikard, Andrew. "Do I Own My Domain if You Grade It?" *EdSurge.* 10 August 2015.

Robertson, Tara. "A Feminist Among Us: An Interview with Chris Bourg." *Feminists Among Us: Resistance and Advocacy in Library Leadership.* Litwin Books. 2017.

Sackstein, Starr. *Hacking Assessment: 10 Ways to Go Gradeless in a Traditional Grades School.* Times 10 Publications, 2015.

Schinske, Jeffrey, and Kimberly Tanner. "Teaching More by Grading Less (or Differently)." *CBE—Life Sciences Education.* Vol. 13, no. 2., 2014.

Sharma, Amarendra and Abigail Carr. "Food Insecurity and Standardized Test Scores." *SSRN.* 26 July 2015.

Stommel, Jesse. "Care is a Practice; Care is Pedagogical." *Academe.* Vol. 106, no. 4, 2020.

Stommel, Jesse. "Critical Digital Pedagogy: a Definition." *Hybrid Pedagogy.* 17 November 2014.

Stommel, Jesse. "The Human Work of Higher Education Pedagogy." *Academe*. Vol. 106, no. 1, 2020.

Stommel, Jesse. "The Moment That Changed the Way I Teach." *The Chronicle of Higher Education*. 5 December 2018.

Swauger, Shea. "Our Bodies Encoded: Algorithmic Test Proctoring in Higher Education." *Hybrid Pedagogy*. 2 April 2020.

Thoreau, Henry David. *On the Duty of Civil Disobedience*. 1849.

Waters, Audrey. "From Open to Justice." *Hack Education*. 16 November 2014.

Woolf, Virginia. *A Room of One's Own*. Harcourt, 1929.

## PREVIOUS PUBLICATIONS

"I Would Prefer Not To" appeared on Hybrid Pedagogy in 2014.

"An Introduction to Ungrading" is adapted from presentation notes published in 2021 at jessestommel.com.

"Why I Don't Grade" appeared in 2017 at jessestommel.com and was adapted in 2020 for *Ungrading: Why Rating Students Undermines Learning (and What to Do Instead)* edited by Susan D. Blum.

"Learning is Not a Mechanism" appeared on Hybrid Pedagogy in 2015. The publication there was adapted from a piece published on Educating Modern Learners.

"Love and Other Data Assets" appeared in Vol. 32, no. 2 of *Against the Grain*.

"If bell hooks Made a Learning Management System" appeared in 2017 at jessestommel.com.

"Grades are Dehumanizing: Ungrading is No Simple Solution" appeared in 2021 at *Times Higher Ed*.

"How to Ungrade" appeared in 2018 at jessestommel.com and was adapted in 2020 for *Ungrading: Why Rating Students Undermines Learning (and What to Do Instead)* edited by Susan D. Blum.

"Compassionate Grading Policies" appeared in 2022 at jessestommel.com.

"Frequently Asked Questions" appeared in 2020 at jessestommel.com.

"What if We Didn't Grade?: A Bibliography" appeared in 2020 at jessestommel.com.

"Do We Need the Word 'Ungrading'?" appeared in an open-access special issue from *Zeal: a Journal for the Liberal Arts*.

www.ingramcontent.com/pod-product-compliance
Lightning Source LLC
Chambersburg PA
CBHW050638160426
43194CB00010B/1721